SIGNS OF HOPE

DEVELOPING SMALL CHRISTIAN COMMUNITIES

James O'Halloran, SDB

Maryknoll, New York 10545

Published by Orbis Books, Maryknoll, N.Y. 10545
Manufactured in the United States of America

Published in Ireland by The Columba Press, 93, The Rise, Mount Merrion, Blackrock, Co. Dublin.

Library of Congress Cataloging-in-Publication Data

O'Halloran, James.
Signs of hope: developing small Christian Communities / James O'Halloran.
p. cm.
Rev. and expanded ed. of: Living cells.
Includes bibliographical references.
ISBN 0-88344-730-4
1. Christian communities—Catholic Church. 2. Catholic Church—Developing countries. I. O'Halloran, James. Living cells. II. Title.
BX2347.7.0385 1990
250—dc20 90-46180
CIP

ORBIS/ISBN 0-88344-730-4
The Columba Press ISBN 1 85607 0107

For all those people, whatever their convictions,
who are everywhere gathering in small communities
to build a better world.

Contents

Introduction

There is a story told of a tourist who was travelling through rural Ireland and wasn't quite sure of his bearings. He therefore asked a farmer, working in a nearby field, if he were on the correct road to Askeaton. Wishing to be courteous and as kind as possible in the circumstances to the tourist, the farmer replied, "Well, you're on the right road to Askeaton all right. It's just that you're facin' in the wrong direction."

This volume is not a handbook. However, I hope that it provides some guidelines, or signposts, that may at least keep people who are developing small Christian communities facing in the right general direction. It builds on *Living Cells* which very many people have found helpful in their efforts to establish small Christian communities. It is the product of being part of the small Christian community experience for twenty years as member, resource person, and animator. It is also shaped by much feedback on former writings. I would hope, then, that it might prove a useful resource for theological reflection and pastoral practice. The practical, or pastoral, nature of the book will be quite evident from the table of contents.

Instead of using the "he/she" form, for the most part I try to vary the personal pronoun from one part of the book to another.

I should like to thank all those members of small Christian communities who shared with me over the past twenty years. This is their book. For there are not any experts on small Christian communities: only little people with little experiences to share. Finally, I should like to express my gratitude to Beverly Sperry, who works wonders on her computer.

1

The Origins and Nature of Small Christian Communities

In the early 1960s Pearl, a frail little old lady in her 70s, was demonstrating outside the White House against racism. She was arrested and imprisoned. While in prison she had a heart attack, but refused to go to the nearest hospital because it did not admit black people. And having survived the prison and the heart attack, back she went to demonstrate against racism in front of the White House.

Twenty years later I met Pearl at a meeting protesting the nuclear threat. To me she seemed a most experienced, wise and holy person. So I thought I would put an important question, perhaps the most important question, to her. "Pearl," I asked, "what is happiness?"

Without hesitation, out of her long experience and great wisdom, she replied, "Happiness is *belonging*."

How right she was. Happiness is belonging to a family where I am loved and accepted as I am. Happiness is belonging to a community where I am loved and accepted as I am. Even the happiness of heaven consists in being absorbed into the community of the Trinity. Hence the relevance of the small Christian communities, or basic Christian communities, that have appeared in the Church over recent decades.

ORIGINS

While small Christian communities are an entirely new experience of Church, it is possible to identify them in a special way with some New Testament communities. The American Scripture scholar, Raymond Brown, has made us aware that even in New Testament times the Church expressed itself in diverse forms. He points to seven distinct models of Church among the early Christians.[1] They are as follows:

- The heritage that Paul leaves us in the pastoral epistles of Titus and 1 and 2 Timothy. This model emphasizes Church organization. Authority is important and, consequently, the role of presbyter-bishop is stressed.
- Then there is the model that considers the Church as Christ's body to be loved. This can be found in Colossians and Ephesians and is also traced to Paul.
- From the Gospel of Luke and Acts we get a third Pauline model, namely, the Church and the Spirit. This highlights the presence and action of the Spirit.
- In 1 Peter we find the Petrine heritage of the Church seen as people of God. This is a model that makes one feel a strong sense of belonging.
- There is the tradition of John in the Fourth Gospel. This tradition shows people as a community of disciples personally attached to Jesus.
- John provides a further model in his epistles. It is a community of individuals guided by the Paraclete-Spirit.
- And finally there is the heritage of Jewish-Gentile Christians in the Gospel of Matthew. This emphasizes an "authority that does not stifle Jesus."

This Jewish-Gentile heritage also reminds us of another fact. The early Christian communities learned much from the Jewish synagogue. The synagogue taught them to be real expressions of the culture of their time. And it helped them to be effective means for gathering people together to communicate with them and, through them, with others.

Among the early Christians, then, the Church expressed itself in a variety of ways. If we consider the foregoing models, we shall realize that modern small Christian communities resonate in a special way with some of them. These communities could readily relate to the body-of-Christ model of Colossians and Ephesians, the Pauline Church and the Spirit heritage from the Gospel of Luke and Acts, the people-of-God tradition from

1 Peter, John's Gospel model of a community of disciples personally attached to Jesus and the tradition of a community of individuals guided by the Paraclete-Spirit found in the epistles of John.

Yet even in the models of Matthew's Gospel and the Pastoral Epistles where authority and organization were important, authority was not authoritarian, organization was not overweening and the voice of the laity was not unheard—it was crucial in decision making.

With the coming of the Roman Emperor Constantine (288?–337) the Church ceased to be persecuted and Christianity became the favored religion of the Empire. It was fashionable to be Christian and the Church greatly increased in numbers. However, it lost the momentum of a Church that had until then been lean, persecuted and more committed. The edge of witness became blunted. In the mid fourth century bishops were installed as public officials. This engendered a Church model that was both hierarchical and institutional, a model that prevailed as the communitarian vision faded.

The neighborhood community, or house church (*oikos*), ceased to be and the focus came to be placed on parish and diocese. With the departure of the small neighborhood community, a dimension which gave the early Church much of its vitality was gone. And, truth to tell, the Church has never been quite the same without that dimension. But in our own day ordinary Christians are reclaiming their heritage, as small Christian communities increase in number around the world. That Christians enjoy this heritage, this full experience of the Kingdom, is not something granted to them by favor but is theirs by right. It cannot be denied them and, if it is, they must assert their right, for "the kingdom of God has suffered violence, and the violent take it by force" (Matthew 11:12).

MODERN TIMES

There seems to be general agreement that in our time the small Christian communities began in Brazil in the mid-fifties. Leonardo Boff traces their beginning to the lament of a humble old woman. If it is so, her words may turn out to be among the most momentous uttered in Church history. "Christmas Eve," she complained, "all three Protestant churches were lit up and full of people. . . . And the Catholic church closed and dark! . . . Because we can't get a priest."[2] The question naturally arose as to why everything should come to a standstill simply because there was no priest. This led to an initiative by Dom Agnello Rossi, prelate of Rio de Janeiro at the time, to establish a community evangelization movement in Barra do Pirai, Rio de Janeiro.

> Specific concerns [explains Boff] were with a movement for grass-roots community catechetics and general education via radio, from Natal, Rio de Janeiro, and various lay apostolate experiments and parish renewal within the framework of a renewal movement projected in the national pastoral plans (1962–65).[3]

That was in 1956.

From Brazil, the small communities spread to Chile, Honduras, Panama and with time to all Latin America and even the world beyond. This growth was greatly encouraged by the meetings of the Latin American bishops at Medellín, Colombia, in 1968, and at Puebla, Mexico, in 1979. Estimates state that there are between 180,000 and 200,000 such communities in Latin America.[4] More than half of these are in Brazil.

As we approach the third millennium, however, we can really regard the small Christian communities as a world phenomenon. They are to be found by the thousands in Africa, Asia (in the Philippines, Indonesia, Papua New Guinea and China), Europe (Eastern and Western) and in the United States. In the United States they are to be encountered especially, though not solely, among peoples of Hispanic origins. Statistics are taken only sporadically. Apart from those given above, there are an estimated 10,000 small Christian communities in East Africa alone and one in ten parishes have identifiable small Christian communities in South Africa.[5] But it has not been a major concern of those involved in this new and helpful initiative to stop and count groups.

Of course bishops in Africa have been encouraging the establishment of small Christian communities. AMECEA (Association of Member Episcopal Conferences in Eastern Africa) prelates made their establishment a priority at Nairobi (1976) and renewed their intent in Malawi (1979). SECAM (the Symposium of Episcopal Conferences in Africa and Madagascar) has also been fostering them: at Yaondé (1981) and Kinshasa (1984). The Kinshasa meeting had this to say:

> We recommend to Episcopal Conferences, Assemblies and Associations in Africa:
>
> (1) to do all they can to encourage the emergence of a pastoral plan for "Small Christian Communities" or "Small Ecclesial Communities" that are able to undertake integrated activities of evangelization and development.[6]

The small Christian communities, or basic Christian communities, have been described in Church documents as "a source of hope for the universal Church"[7] and "causes of joy and hope in the Church."[8] Nevertheless, there are many who have heard little as to what they are all about. Having worked with and been part of the communities for twenty years, I find myself stressing what follows.[9]

A LIVING CELL

A small Christian community is

- Usually a group consisting of eight to thirty persons related to a specific area or neighborhood (also found in schools and universities).
- A group whose members
  - share the same faith in Jesus the Savior,
  - relate the word of God to life (its problems/opportunities) and life to the word of God,
  - and reach out a helping hand to others, especially those whom society pushes aside.
- A group of persons who relate deeply to one another and fit into a community vision of the Church.
- A group that, as it matures, begins to acquire the characteristics of the universal Church, namely, faith, love, worship,

mission, prophecy (concern for justice), service, animation/coordination and communion with pastors. In other words it is a group that makes real the saving will of God in the world. The Church's universality comes not from being a far-flung organization, but from possessing the foregoing features. In this sense even a local small Christian community is universal in nature.

There is a helpful analogy regarding the small community possessing all the characteristics of the universal Church. In a loaf of bread we find a variety of ingredients: flour, salt, water, yeast. Now, if we break off a tiny piece, we find the exact same ingredients in the piece as in the entire loaf. Just so, the small Christian community has all the ingredients—characteristics—of the universal Church.

We are talking really of a group that is an integral part, a living cell, of the Church. In 1968, the Latin American bishops at Medellín described it as the Church in nucleus.[10] The word "nucleus" implies that we are talking of a core group that influences outwards and rallies inwards and of a group that is the Church in miniature. Both Paul VI[11] and John Paul II[12] have insisted that the small Christian communities are cells of the Church. They can say this precisely because the communities have the characteristics of the universal Church and make available, or incarnate, the saving will of God in history. That the small communities are integral parts of the Church was a point also made by the Special Synod of Bishops, Rome, in 1985. It declared:

> Since the Church is a communion, the new "Basic Communities" as they are called are a true expression of communion, and an instrument for fashioning a more profound communion, provided they live in genuine unity with the Church. They are thus a sign of great hope in the life of the Church.[13]

In an interview at Crumlin, Dublin, in 1979, Cardinal Silva Henriquez of Santiago, Chile, gave a good thumbnail sketch of what small Christian community is. And he also showed how much the Latin American bishops pin their hopes upon it:

> The small Christian community has served us wonderfully well in Latin America. That subcontinent created and continues to support and direct such groups. The small community is a living cell within the Church; a small-scale group with human warmth; a group in which the Gospel can be lived totally; a nucleus that projects itself into the wider community, be it parish or diocese. A cell such as this will be an effective instrument of evangelization and will transform world structures that are nowadays so materialistic. This is a noble ideal; an ideal which the Latin American bishops hope to achieve through the small communities. Perhaps there is something in this for Ireland.[14]

We have stressed that the small Christian communities are truly ecclesial, or cells of the Church. We did so because not all movements or groups that participate in the life of the Church, and enrich it with their charism, are integral parts of the Church's being. The Church existed long before any of them was founded.

Now as the small Christian communities multiply and develop

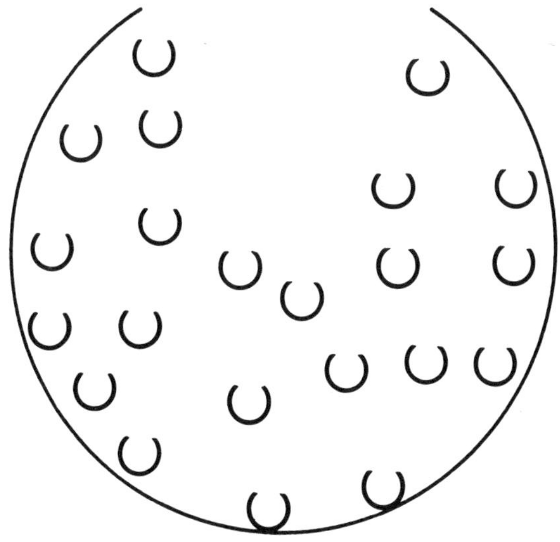

in a parish, through their openness to each other and all the Christians of an area, they can quietly transform the parish. The parish then becomes a *communion of communities*.

The most effective way to renew a parish is to make it a communion of communities. As the communities gain representation at the parish center, on the parish council for example, they energize the center and are in turn energized by it. In *Evangelii Nuntiandi*, Paul VI noted the significance of the small groups for the wider community.[15] He realized their powerful potential for influencing outwards and rallying inwards.

There is a parish in an African town where the small communities have been functioning for the past several years. At the end of the first year they were evaluating their progress. They felt they had quite a way to go in the areas of formation and community-building. They were pleased, however, that even in a short time the groups had strengthened the spirit of the community in the parish.

Of course these are still early days for the small Christian communities and it is difficult to say how they may network in the years ahead. Will the existing parish serve as the basis for the communion of communities? Or will some entirely new entity emerge? It is difficult to say. There is evidence certainly that an existing parish can successfully function as a communion of communities. Boundaries might have to soften, however, and room be left for overlapping and adjustment. Developments may with time even lead to an entirely new format.

If our parishes truly take on the aspect of communion, then the diocese can be considered a communion of parishes, the worldwide Church a communion of dioceses. And all these communions should be immersed in the world, enhancing the human/Christian values that are to be found there. The diagram on top of page 11 may help to illustrate our points.

Needless to say, this scheme of things blurs physically once one gets beyond the parish.

I feel I should explore somewhat further the topic of dynamism in the small Christian community. With its commitment to Christ and Gospel/human values it should galvanize larger Christian communities, communities of other religions and those who profess no particular religion at all.

For the sake of argument let us suppose that there is a street, village, or area of 500 inhabitants. Let us further suppose that there are 150 Christians in the place under consideration and that 20 belong to the small Christian community. The influence of the 20 should ripple out to the remaining Christians and to all the others as well.

I have recently returned from Ghana and Sierra Leone where

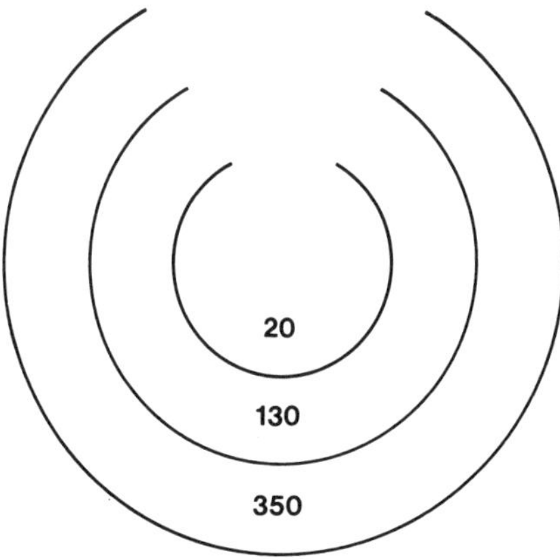

I was sharing insights and experiences on the subject of small Christian communities with persons who were hoping to start them. At the same time I encountered some groups that had resulted from a similar initiative seven years ago, and there was an aspect of them that struck me forcibly. It relates to what has just been said about outreach. Normally I have thought of outreach in terms of *influencing outwards*, yet I became aware in Ghana that *rallying inwards* is also a way of making an impact.

The small Christian communities were rallying points for all the surrounding people, Christians and other. Not all the Christians attended the weekly meetings of the small communities and this worried some of the leaders. But I pointed out to one group that if the 100 or so Christians who lived in the area all came to the community, it would no longer be "small." However, the constant group of 20 proved a rallying point for the surrounding people.

And so it was with all the small communities. When the priest came to celebrate a monthly Eucharist, the members would gather all the Christians, who came gladly. They marshalled Christians to look after the sick and bury the dead, an act of profound religious and cultural significance in Africa. When the small Christian communities went to the main parish church for some celebration, all the surrounding Christians wanted to accompany "our small Christian community," as they called the group with which they identified. Similarly, the surrounding people, Christian and other, cooperated with the groups when there was a road to be mended, a well to be sunk, public conveniences to be built, trees to be planted. In one area a leader of a small Christian community was elected as a representative to the local council. Those who elected him were for the most part Muslim. This is surely a sign of hope in our times. We are all of course saved in community, but, it would appear, there are various ways of belonging.

In short, then, the small Christian community is a living cell of the Church with the power to communicate life to larger groups.

COMMITMENT

Commitment is the mainspring of genuine Christian outreach. And commitment really is the soul of community; by this it will either stand or fall. Commitment means a persevering and total dedication to Christ and Gospel values. There has to be commitment on the part of each member of the community and of the community as a whole.

This of course presupposes conversion—that the members have taken seriously the responsibilities that come with baptism. At some point in their lives they have made a "U-turn" away from evil and towards God. Every day they strive to become a little less selfish, a little more generous. In other words they strive each day to grow in love, which is how we live our faith.

When sharing on this point of conversion with groups, I find it important to remind myself and those to whom I am speaking that this does not mean that a small community is composed of angels. It is composed of sinners who in their brokenness often fall (cf. Proverbs 24:16). Yet they steadfastly refuse to stay down. They always rise again to be reconciled with God and their neighbor. Community is always being built through continual reconciliation. St. John Bosco used to tell his boys that the tragedy lay not in falling, but in failing to rise again. And Dom Helder Camara writes:

> At the great judgment the Lord may say to someone: "How horrible! You fell a million times!" But all is salvaged if that person can say: "Yes, Lord, it really is frightful! But your grace helped me to get back on my feet quickly a million and one times!"[16]

When I think of commitment in connection with small Christian community, people like Miguel often come to mind. From Monday to Saturday he spent long arduous hours working in his South American factory for a paltry wage. He also spent long hours travelling to and fro in overcrowded buses. Yet on Sunday, he labored up the steep slopes of the Andes to give religious education to children who otherwise would go without. "When Sunday comes," he once told me, "I often feel ill and not at all like going up the mountain. But how good the Lord is because, when I overcome my weariness and go, I always feel better." Of such dedicated people, surely, is the Kingdom of God.

SHARING

The supreme Gospel value that impels the committed small Christian community is of course love. The members share all aspects of their lives. It is noteworthy the number of times the word "share" and the allied word "support" are on the lips of small community members. I think we must be careful not to allow these familiar terms to slip by unnoticed. In the latter part of the twentieth century, an age characterized by so much individualism and anonymity, they may be real signs of the times. They may be the new and relevant names for "love," expressing a hunger for community. Quite often when we think of sharing, we think of it simply as a distribution of material goods. But it is much more than that.

The members of the community share spiritually. They worship together: they pray, reflect on the word of God and celebrate the Eucharist. They share intuitions, fantasies, dreams and ideas. They share feelings and friendship. Whatever work (apostolate) the group does they also share, and of course they share material goods.

In short, the participants share all aspects of their lives: spiritual, intuitive, imaginative, intellectual, emotional, apostolic and material.

I once came across an impressive example of sharing by a small Christian community on the edge of a big African city. There was a crotchety, yet destitute, man who was helped by the group. Among other things the community built him a little house. Not long afterwards it was burned down.

Some members of the community resisted the idea of rebuilding it. After all, they reasoned, why help such a thankless old sinner? There were even whisperings that he himself had burned down the house.

One of the members objected to this attitude within the community. "Are we only going to help nice people then?" he asked. "Is that what Christianity is about?" That of course is not what Christianity is about. Rather it is about loving everyone, even an enemy.

The Christian may burn with indignation at the ravaging of

the environment, the nuclear threat or the enslavement of humans by humans, yet may not use any cause, however just, as an excuse to hate.

By the way, the little house was rebuilt.

PRAYER AND ACTION

The spirituality of the small Christian community is an integral spirituality that combines prayer and action. Neither aspect is neglected and this is important, because a spirituality that tries to function either on the basis of prayer or action alone is a spirituality that tries to fly on one wing. Sooner or later it will falter.

In recent years we have become more and more conscious that the word of God must be life-related. That is, it must be put into practice. Equally, I feel, must we put prayer into practice. Maybe this is not quite so obvious. It is easy to equate long hours spent in prayer with holiness. And yet prayer, no matter how prolonged, that does not issue in action is spurious.

Mystics, above all, realize that prayer and action are essential ingredients of a true spirituality—two aspects of the same reality. We recall the words of the boy Teddy in the story of that name by J. D. Salinger. On one occasion Teddy, on seeing his little sister drink milk, realized with a blinding insight "that *she* was God and the *milk* was God."[17] Thus the step from mysticism to reality is a short one. Teresa of Avila used to say, "The Lord walks among the pots and pans."[18] And the step from mysticism to social concern is also a short one. Although a monk, Thomas Merton was one of the first to condemn the Vietnam war. He wrote:

> But "no man is an island." A purely individualistic inner life, unconcerned for the suffering of others, is unreal. Therefore my meditation on love and peace must be realistically and intimately related to the fury of war, bloodshed, burning, destruction, killing that takes place on the other side of the earth.[19]

The most common form of prayer practiced in the small Christian community is that which comes straight from the heart.

Usually this spontaneous prayer flows from a life-related reflection on the word of God and is broken by moments of silent meditation. Spontaneity in this case certainly does not mean a thoughtless blurting out of sentiments; the term simply means that no set or formal prayers are used.

Following a reflection on Matthew 25:31–46 ("I was hungry and you gave me food, I was thirsty and you gave me drink"), for example, someone might pray like this:

> Almighty God, help me and all of our community to realize the dignity of every human being, without exception. Jesus considers as done to himself whatever we do to even the least of our sisters and brothers. Help me, Lord, to treat all your people with reverence and respect. May I assist them when they are in need.

And after a reflection on Luke 24:13–35, which treats of the two disciples on the way to Emmaus, I once heard a simple woman in a Latin American *barrio*, or poor area, pray somewhat as follows:

> Almighty God, it was only when bread was broken that the disciples knew Jesus. They recognized him in the breaking of bread, an act of sharing, an act of love; and that was because God is love and Jesus is the Son of God. When we love, we make the Trinity present in the world. Almighty God, help us to love.

If I hadn't known that Laura made that prayer, I might have thought that it came from Teresa of Avila. But Laura composed it.

Many of the spontaneous prayers quite rightly center around the concerns of people's lives: the recovery of a sick relative, work for the unemployed, success in an examination, freedom from hunger, disease and oppression. And these prayers naturally move the members of communities to action.

The more simple the culture, the more skillful the folk can be at making their own prayers. In the Third World people are often quite at home with spontaneous prayer. By contrast, technically advanced cultures are conditioned by instant tea, instant coffee and microwave ovens. The instant society can fail to understand that a facility for spontaneous prayer cannot be acquired overnight.

An example will help us to realize that there is a process involved. It is taken from a small Christian community in Dublin. When they first started, this group discussed problems a great deal. They tended to shy away from the spiritual. Since they had been formed as a small Christian community, however, the coordinators would read some passage of Scripture related to the problem under consideration. The reading was not an integral part of the meeting, but something of an afterthought that could at a pinch be discarded. And that was how matters stood at the beginning.

After a few sessions the animators commenced to invite all to join hands and recite the Lord's Prayer to finish off the meeting.

Almost imperceptibly some spontaneous prayer crept in. Usually it was the coordinators who tried it. But gradually others began to imitate them and acquire the skill.

Seven years later that same community can put a candle on the floor in the middle of the room, turn out the lights, reflect on the Scriptures and relate them to life and pray spontaneously for an hour, or even two.

Small Christian communities may wish to do a course on prayer. I include some material in the bibliography that animators may find helpful in fostering both community and private prayer.

PRIVATE PRAYER

I once went to a dear, eighty-year-old confessor of mine who in the course of our chat asked these questions:

"How's the prayer goin'?"

"Er ... um ... father ... I've been reading St. Teresa of Avila and St. John of the Cross and—"

"Are you *doin'* it?"

"Well, ... I'm finding Charles de Foucauld's writings also most helpful...."

He guffawed. "Yes, but are you *doin'* it?" he persisted relentlessly.

He then went on to say that there was no alternative to "plonking" ourselves down morning and evening for half an hour or twenty minutes and actually praying.

Of course Father Tom was absolutely right.

Small Christian community members, as well as praying in common, feel a need for private prayer. Whether it be silent meditation or oral is a matter of choice. Words are not even necessary. Commenting on Matthew's phrase, "In your prayers do not babble as the pagans do" (6:7), Charles de Foucauld says:

> In this counsel you [God] are telling us that for mental prayer *words are not necessary*: it is enough to kneel there lovingly at Your feet, contemplating Your majesty with every admiration, every desire for your glory, consolation and love, in short with every movement of our hearts that love prompts us to. Prayer, as St. Theresa tells us, consists *in not speaking a lot*, but in loving a lot.[20]

In short, we could define prayer as thinking of God with affection.

There are those who find it helpful to pray by reciting a mantra such as *Maranatha* (Come, Lord Jesus) over and over again, as a means of focusing the attention on God. They usually do this sitting in an upright position, breathing evenly and with eyes closed.

The mystics seem to experience God directly and this is not the result of a great deal of rationalizing. They have the deep intuition, already referred to, that all reality is one in the end, and they try to tune into this harmony. It has been thought that only persons such as Teresa of Avila and John of the Cross are favored with mystical experiences, but there is no convincing reason to believe that these experiences are not the lot of many quite ordinary people.

Of course the real truth about the world and all things in it, including humans, is that they are God's creation and therefore graced and good. This is why a truly religious person is always a confirmed optimist. Sinfulness has marred, yet not destroyed, the goodness of the world. So in a sense the whole universe is a sacrament of God. That is to say, it speaks to us of God's presence and graciousness. Looking into a bluebell may be a way of looking into the depths of God's being.

I well remember a moonlit night, diamond sharp and clear, that I once spent in the Andes. Snow-capped Cotopaxi was palely visible and the stars at that altitude were sparkling peep-holes in the floor of heaven. Fresh trout for breakfast from a tumbling mountain stream were proof of God's generosity.

But what about the famine-ridden areas of the world, some may wonder. Why doesn't God provide some trout for those? There is, of course, enough food on the earth to feed all of its inhabitants, if we were to share it. Do we expect God to provide the organization and transport to do this? Or, as co-creators with God, must we too not play our part? Doesn't the compassion of God shine through the work that UNICEF does for the hapless children of the planet? And isn't the courage of its Executive Director, James Grant, admirable when he declares:

> When the impact [of the third-world debt] becomes visible in rising death rates among children, rising percentages of low birth-weight babies, falls in the average weight-for-height of the under-fives, and falling school enrollment, then it is time to strip away the niceties of economic parlance and say that what has happened is simply an outrage against a large section of humanity.[21]

If we actively responded to the seeds of goodness that God has placed in all our hearts, justice would become the prevailing reality in the world and gratuitous suffering a distant memory.

So when the members of a small Christian community communicate their Christian, or human, values to the world, those values will strike a sympathetic chord in society. They already exist there. The sacred–profane division is spurious. God is present in history. However, by abusing our freedom, we can get in the way of divine purposes.

ACTION

The question often arises as to what sort of action a small Christian community should undertake. Firstly the members, simply by being what they are, ought to bring Gospel values, or basic human values, to those places where their daily activities take them: the teacher to the school, the nurse to the hospital, the young person to the youth club, the politician to the parliament, the factory worker to the factory, the business person to the shop. . . . In *Populorum Progressio* Paul VI calls upon Catholics the world over, "without waiting passively for orders or directives, to take the initiative freely and to infuse a Christian spirit into the mentality, customs, laws and structures of the community in which they live."[22] Again it is not a case of the Christian bringing virtue to an utterly corrupt world. The seeds of goodness are already there.

In other words the Church must be in history and not cut off from it. Too often we have erected barriers between faith and practice, religion and life, the Church and history.

FAITH	PRACTICE
RELIGION	LIFE
CHURCH	HISTORY

A story of a novice from my own seminary days illustrates this mentality. He fell ill in the course of the novitiate and the doctor was summoned. The doctor was a large, good-natured man but professed no religion.

He inquired of the novice if he had ever had the illness before.

To which the novice replied that he had had "a touch of it"—when he was in the world.

There was a long baffled pause. Then the doctor casually inquired, "As a matter of interest, where the devil do you think you are now?"

Not only will the members of small Christian communities give witness to Gospel values in their places of study, work or leisure, but they will also take their skills back to their homes and neighborhoods. If a member is a nurse and a neighbor's child is ill, he will call to see if there isn't something he can do. As will be evident from the experiences of small communities to be given later (see chapters 5 and 6), in effect members are deeply involved in their neighborhoods: providing religious education, working with young people, conducting courses, visiting those with problems, engaging in development work, being active in the cause of justice and peace.

A small community really should have a plan of action. The members ought to do something in the name of the community and be accountable to it for what they do, not so much as a check, but rather as a support. When they can talk about their difficulties and are upheld by the prayers and concern—even the active help—of their friends, it is of enormous help.

And if it be possible for them to work in teams rather than as individuals, so much the better. Jesus sent out his apostles to teach two by two, not alone. "For," as he says in Matthew's Gospel, "where two or three are gathered in my name, there am I in the midst of them" (18:20).

In the complicated world of today it is not usually possible for all the members of a community to be engaged in the same task. If on occasions, however, they can all join together in doing something, it is a marvelous help towards developing community. All the works done in the name of community, whether by individuals or teams, contribute greatly towards creating a community spirit.

In the beginning a community will respond to some obvious needs around it. With time as it gains in strength and consistency, the members may become more thoroughgoing in their approach. This could entail making an analysis of their area in an effort to get at the needs and problems as seen by the ordinary people of the place (see chapter 9).

Action must always be reflected upon. There has to be constant interplay between action and reflection:

ACTION <------------------------- REFLECTION
------------------------->

We shall return to this later.

In short, then, prayer and action are vital for a small Christian community. If either is missing, the spirituality limps. A way of life that integrates prayer and action is on the contrary complete. It also reflects the life of Christ who not only went to the mountaintop and desert to pray, but also travelled about doing good, bringing love and healing to many.

CONCLUSION

In the present chapter we have seen some of the major features of small Christian community; and the whole work that follows is devoted to deepening our knowledge of the phenomenon. However, one cannot package small Christian community, tie a ribbon on it and present it to someone. As we shall see, it shares in the mystery that is God and as such cannot be defined.

SUMMARY

1. Happiness is belonging.
2. The small Christian communities find their origins in the New Testament.
3. With the coming of Constantine (288?–377) a hierarchical/institutional model of Church prevailed.
4. There is general agreement that in modern times the small Christian communities originated in Brazil and from there spread to the remainder of Latin America (cf. Note 9 for a contrary view).
5. They have now become a world phenomenon.
6. Small Christian community is usually a group consisting of eight to thirty members, related to a specific area or neighborhood (it is also to be found in schools and universities). It is a group whose members relate deeply, share the same faith in Jesus the Savior and relate worship and the word of God to life—by concerning itself with others, especially those whom society pushes aside. It does this through a process of influencing outwards and rallying inwards. And finally it is a group that is an integral part, or cell, of the Church, fitting into a community model of Church.
7. The commitment of each member and of the community as a whole is the soul of small Christian community.

8. The participants share all aspects of their lives: spiritual, intuitive, imaginative, intellectual, emotional, apostolic, material.
9. The spirituality of the small Christian community is integral, or one. It has two facets: prayer and action.

Please note that an appropriate query for discussion at the end of each chapter in this book would be:

WHAT QUESTIONS AND ISSUES DID THE FOREGOING CHAPTER RAISE FOR YOU?

Striving to relate what has been said to one's own experience is of vital importance.

Bible passages relevant to the questions and issues are found in Appendix 1.

2

The Church as Communion

A senior citizen in a parish I know felt it was "an awful shame" that the Church didn't wait until all the old people were dead before bringing in the changes made by Vatican II. There is a point here. Like that person, we have all felt, and are still feeling, the repercussions of the Council. We feel this not only in the Church but even more significantly in the world.

Having considered some of the major features of small Christian community, I need hardly add that it is not a reality isolated from Vatican II. The Council gave us a new vision of the Church as community, new at least for our times. So the Church is a communion with ever-increasing lay involvement in all facets of its life—liturgical, apostolic, administrative. It is a prayerful Church with a missionary concern for the promotion of the Kingdom of God and its justice. The small Christian community gives practical expression to this vision and is also, as we shall see, an instrument for bringing it about.

EXPLORING THE VISION

One of the basic themes of Vatican II was the Church as communion. Speaking of the action of the Spirit, the *Dogmatic Constitution of the Church* (*Lumen Gentium*) has this to say:

> Guiding the Church in the way of all truth (cf. Jeremiah 16:13) and *unifying her in communion* and in the works of

> ministry, he [the Spirit] bestows upon her varied hierarchic and charismatic gifts, and in this way directs her and leads her to *perfect union* with her Spouse. For the Spirit and the bride both say to Jesus, the Lord, "Come" (cf. Revelation 22:17). Hence the universal Church is seen to be "*a people brought into unity from the unity of the Father, the Son and the Holy Spirit*" (italics mine).[23]

The Special Synod of Bishops (Rome, 1985), quoted above, also refers explicitly to the Church as communion. Gatherings such as the Council and Synod drew our attention to the Church as people of God rather than as buildings and organization. The Church community comprises laity and clergy. They complement each other and through baptism are fundamentally equal. Because of ordination, the bishop, priest and deacon are appointed by the community (guided by the Spirit) to exercise among other tasks an animating or leadership role. Leadership, however, is for service, not for lording it over people. And the leadership of the clergy does not at all rule out leadership among the laity.

In many parts of the world the Church is viewed as a steeple which may be seen from afar (if it isn't blocked out by high-rise buildings); it is understood as the pastor associated with the steeple, and the surrounding, well-defined, often jealously guarded geographic area.

But as Bob Dylan used to sing, "the times they are a-changin'." Many Christians can now understand the story of a priest who was visiting a fellow priest in the sprawling *barrio* of a Latin American city. He travelled by bus to the area, got off and began scanning the horizon for a church steeple which he felt would be highly visible. So he started to walk . . . and walk. Still no steeple. With night falling, he entered a shop and asked the woman behind the counter if she could tell him where the Church of Our Lady of Guadalupe was.

She thought for a moment, then answered, "It's Thursday. They will be gathering this evening at the Sanchez home." For her the Church was quite definitely a community of disciples.

FROM COMMUNITY TO TRINITY

If we look at the small Christian community in practice, what do we find? A group of people who, because of their faith in Christ and efforts to love and share, *are one*. However imperfectly. I believe that in the end we must look for the roots of this harmony in the Blessed Trinity. So from the existing small community let us move to the Trinity and the steps by which we arrive at this conclusion.

Within the Trinity we have the Father, Son and Holy Spirit—three persons—who through their infinite loving and sharing are confessed to be one God, or one Community. *God then is community*. From all eternity it has been so.

In Africa when treating of the Trinity, they say there are three dancers but only one dance. This is a rather interesting way of explaining the bond and, whether or not people are aware of it, not without a historical foundation. The Greeks in the early Church used the word *choreuein* (to dance) in an effort to describe how the persons of the Trinity related to one another. And it is from *choreuein* that we get the English word "choreography," that is, the arranging or designing of ballet or stage dance. Can we visualize the Trinity as a dynamic trio moving gracefully through eternity, luring all of us, their fellow dancers, to follow?

CREATION

God is one. And God is community. Yet this community proved to be open and did not keep infinite love pent up within itself. That great love burst upon the world in creation. God, Community, created our world and, because it was created by God, it is good, harmonious and graced (see Genesis 1 and 2).

Last, but by no means least, of all living creatures God created human beings "in the divine image" as "male and female" (Genesis 1:26–27). The spelling out of the fact that we were created male and female is significant. There exists here the notion of plurality or community. This, coupled with our being created in God's image, suggests that we are particularly like

God when we live a life of loving and sharing in community as do Father, Son and Spirit.

Humans, therefore, were created as a community of brothers and sisters without divisions, which for me is one of the best descriptions of the Kingdom of God. God could not have created divisiveness, which is negative. From the beginning to the end of the world the intention of God that we be a community of brothers and sisters without divisions never changes. This state of affairs, found in Genesis, we also find in the New Testament. In Galatians 3:28 Paul says: "There does not exist among you Jew or Greek, slave or freeman, male or female. All are one in Christ Jesus." The inference is that there must be no barriers between people on grounds of race, calling, sex, color, religion or whatever.

God of course created us free, and we abused that freedom. Through sin the human community was riven within itself and estranged from God.

JESUS THE LIBERATOR

Sin, however, did not have the last word. When the time was ripe, God sent the only begotten Son, Jesus Christ, to the world as Liberator. This Jesus is the sacrament of the Triune God; that is, through his visible person he makes the invisible God, who is community, present. He is the Emmanuel, or "God with us" (Matthew 1:23).

A friend of mine was giving a workshop to a group of simple people in rural Africa and was asking what Jesus meant to them. An old farmer present answered, "Even before we hear about Christ, our fathers believe in God, we believe in God. The God the missionaries talk about is not the white man's God. There's only one God. He is the same God we always believe in—only we don't know him very well. Now we know more about God, because Jesus is God dressed like a man, and he works with his hands ... like us ... that's very good ... he works with his hands. ..." For this old man, Jesus was truly the Emmanuel, or "God with us" (Matthew 1:23). The faith basis, or theology, by which he lived was indeed profound.

The figure of Jesus is so central to the whole story of community that we must dwell on him somewhat. He is a human way of being divine. So when he forgives sins, heals the broken in mind or body and pleads for widows, orphans, and all those treated unjustly, he reflects the compassion of God to the world. His whole life was a reaching out to others, especially to those whom society pushes aside, so much so that he can accurately be described as a *person for others*.

Jesus' greatest concern and one about which he preached increasingly was the Kingdom – the urgent need for the reign of God to prevail in the world. He remained faithful to his *Abba* (Daddy) in all his words and deeds and tried to draw all people to this loving Father. He ate with persons whom society considered of no account, because he felt called to bring all people into the Kingdom. Jesus obviously loved to eat with friends and tell stories or parables. This eating with tax-collectors and sinners and those parables that often hit hard at the leaders of Israel aroused the suspicion and anger of the powers-that-be. These activities together with a seeming flaunting of the law made his death inevitable. The last straw for the leaders seems to have been the Temple incident, when he drove out those buying and selling and prevented people from carrying anything through the Temple courtyards (cf. Matthew 21:12–17; Mark 11:15–19; Luke 19:45–48; John 2:13–25).

As the end approached, Jesus did what he had done so often in life – sat down to a meal with his friends. And so his life that was for others was symbolized or expressed in a meal. Then the act of complete self-giving that was a feature of the meal was repeated on the cross the following day. Sharing meals with others had been an example of his self-giving throughout the public ministry; it would also be so as death approached. Thus was the meal and the sacrifice on the cross linked forever in the Christian memory. And the whole story was given a dimension beyond the present life when Jesus said to his disciples at the Last Supper: "I tell you I shall not drink again of this fruit of the vine until that day when I drink it new with you in my Father's Kingdom" (Matthew 26:29).

Hanging on the cross, Jesus felt desolate and abandoned, though in reality God never abandoned him. Through Jesus God entered history and suffered the pain of the cross. God shared, in some real fashion, in our human lot of suffering—so much for the myth of a God that is distant and uncaring. In the desolation of Christ God risked failure. But Jesus did not fail. As he passed painfully through the gap of death, Jesus clung with his fingernails to hope. He trusted in his *Abba* and in the promise of the Kingdom, the Kingdom that he had so convincingly preached about, and bore witness to, in the course of his ministry. And God vindicated his trust and the whole purpose of his life by raising him up. The cross represents what we did to Jesus; the resurrection what God did.

In a manner that no other person ever can or ever will express, Jesus shows how God loves us. Jesus is God's way of saying to the world: "I love you." And in a way that could never be undone, Jesus responded in hope and trust to that love. The response of Jesus to the offer of God's love was so complete and final that it brought liberation to the people of every era. He was divine yet also one of us. If we remain faithful in word and deed as we go through life, and if we hope and trust while passing, painfully perhaps, through the gap of death, we too will be vindicated and raised up by God.

Joy, then, finally wins the day as it always should for the Christian. Christ has conquered sin and death and made it possible for all of us to do the same. Death does not have the last word. It is interesting how the Jesus of early Christian celebrations was viewed. He was not the fearsome judge who so often presides over the entrances to medieval cathedrals, but rather was shown as a joyous and attractive young man whose return is longingly awaited. *Maranatha* was the cry of the communities—"Come, Lord Jesus!" And there we find the root of the current exclamation used in the liturgy:

> Christ has died,
> Christ is risen,
> Christ will come again.

JESUS RECONCILES

The nub of all this for our present purposes is that Jesus made God, Community, incarnate in the world and through his fidelity to and trust in his *Abba* freed us from sin. In other words he reconciled us to ourselves, to God, to one another and to the environment. *He restored community*. Restored that situation whereby once again we have the possibility of becoming a community of brothers and sisters without divisions, as envisaged in Genesis 1:26–27.

Jesus, therefore, heals the internal wounds of the human community. He reconciles the human and divine communities. And, furthermore, he reconciles both of these with the community of the rest of creation. In the light of the prevailing concern for the environment, this is surely a most important point. If there isn't what Dr. John Raines of Temple University, Philadelphia, calls "ecological hygiene,"[24] respect for the delicate ecosystem, the result can be disastrous for all living things. It can also adversely affect their relationship with the Creator.

The clearing of the rain forests in the Amazon Basin, for example, has brought us the ominous greenhouse effect that causes severe drought on the one hand; on the other hand, it has led to crime and bloodshed as indigenous human beings, made in God's image, are killed as they defend their traditional hunting and fishing grounds against arbitrary takeover. Quite unlike some humans, God who created everything and found that "it was very good" (Genesis 1:31) treats the environment with loving tenderness:

> Consider the lilies of the field, how they grow; they toil not, neither do they spin; and yet I say unto you, that even Solomon in all his glory was not arrayed like one of these. (Matthew 6:28–29)

CHURCH: THE PRESENCE OF JESUS

Jesus, then, made God present in the world because, where the Son is, there too is the Father and the Spirit. In the Gospel when the apostle Philip asks Jesus to "show us the Father," Jesus replies, "He who has seen me has seen the Father" (John 14:8–9). Jesus also surrounded himself with a community of disciples, so that he became a linch-pin between earthly and divine communities—the point at which they touch.

Christ, however, is no longer with us in the same way as when he was on earth. The Risen Lord does not walk the streets of São Paulo, Nairobi, Melbourne or Manila as the historical Jesus walked the streets of Capernaum in bygone days. Yet he is made present, or incarnate, in all those places through the community of disciples that we call Church. Just as Jesus is the sacrament of God, so the Church is the sacrament of Jesus. This means that as the historical Jesus made the invisible God present in the world, so does the community of disciples that we call Church make the Risen Lord present. In Paul's imagery the Church is the body of Christ (1 Corinthians 12) and in John's a vine of which Jesus is the stock and we are the branches (chapter 15). The Christian community, therefore, as "the body of Christ" can continue Christ's work of promoting the Kingdom through reconciliation and the fostering of harmony in the world. This oftentimes motley gathering of humans that we call "Church" is outward evidence of a glorious treasure within—the permanent offer of grace and salvation for all.

SMALL CHRISTIAN COMMUNITIES

The Church is a worldwide reality that is becoming increasingly hard to identify as the community of Christ's followers or as Christ's presence on earth. It is all too big. The picture is already beginning to blur physically even at the parish stage. One of the places where the Church's true nature and identity with Christ do become clearly apparent is in the small Christian community. If to be Church is to experience—and reflect—the intimate life of loving and sharing that characterizes the Trinity, then this is surely best achieved in small groups. It is difficult in a parish of thousands or for that matter even in a gathering of 100. Hence the relevance of the small community.

A further point. Studying theology and dutifully listening to the teaching of the Church may enlighten us about God. However, it is only by striving to relate intimately as do the Trinity that we can truly come to have any inkling as to who God is. The truth is above all something we *do*.

I recall an African bishop telling me that his diocese had an excellent catechetical program for schools. Much of the effort expended, however, was like putting water into a bucket with a hole in it, because family and community were in disarray. This was because the menfolk, searching for work, migrated to the mining areas of nearby South Africa. Owing to the policy of apartheid they could not bring their wives and children with them. Some never returned; some established a second home in Soweto, Alexandra or wherever. Either way family and community suffered. And what is the good, for example, of telling a child at school that God is love, if love is not experienced in family or small community? It remains a hollow word. The experiential, audio-visual aid of God is missing.

I asked Agnes, a small Christian community member in Ghana, what the group meant to her. The answer was significant: "Formerly when we went to the cathedral on Sunday, you might not know the person beside you. So you didn't experience the same love that you feel in the small Christian community. You see, we know each other well in the group, so the love is more real. I've learned the meaning of Christianity in the group. The priest talked about Christianity in the cathedral, but those were words . . . here it is lived and I understand. I'm very happy."

The foregoing poses some searching questions for all Christians. Can we even begin to think of evangelization and catechesis without the witness of small Christian community, a vital witness to Trinitarian love and harmony and to the oneness of Christ's body? Or what progress do we make in promoting the related realities of development, justice and peace that are rooted in right and intimate relationships? Community is in fact the ground of, and testimony to, all morality.

And, quite apart from the witness aspect of small Christian communities, there is a further nuance: they are also instruments of evangelization, inculturation,[25] catechesis, development, justice and peace, and communication. This, I think, will be made clear by the experiences of chapters 5 and 6 as well as by sundry examples that occur throughout the work.

Although this book is focusing on the subject of the small Christian community, I should like at this point to call attention to the"domestic church,"[26] or family. The relationship of husband and wife is a most wonderful sacrament of God's love. In the intimacy of this relationship the love that exists between

Father, Son and Spirit is powerfully reflected to the world. Reflecting this love of the Trinity in so intense a fashion that two persons become identified as one is surely a marvelous vocation and a unique contribution to Christian spirituality and the well-being of society. Husband and wife constitute a small community and so too does family. If the family is Christian, we are talking of a small Christian community. As compared with the groups we have been speaking about, however, the nuclear family usually has limitations of composition in terms of age, number, occupation, ethnic group, ministry and so forth. The extended family can of course be a different matter. It can offer variety. But the important point is that the family makes incarnate, or real, the love and saving will of God on this earth.

SUMMARY IN DIAGRAM

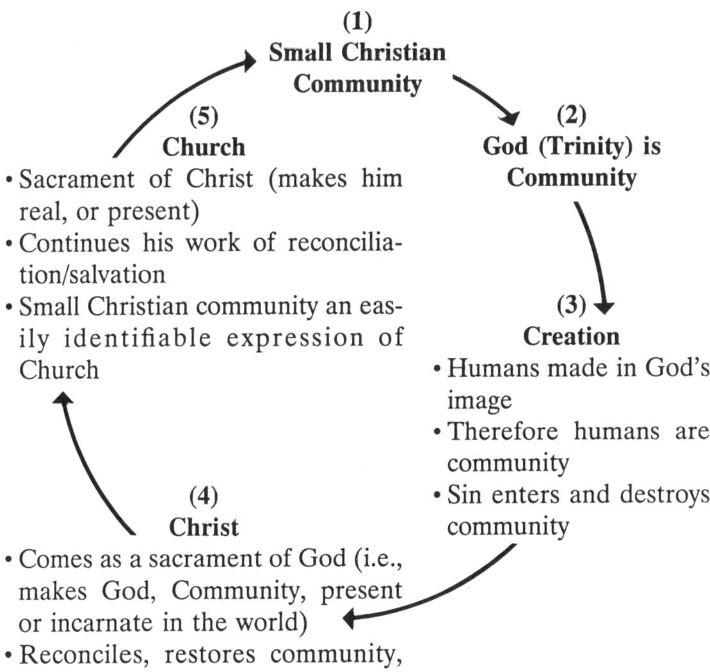

3

The Kingdom of God

"We were like ants in our small Christian communities. We saw our own little patch of ground but not the wider landscape. Now we have a vision. We see where we fit into the Church and the Kingdom and can go forward feeling more confident." So said Peter, a coordinator of a small Christian community, following a workshop in Ghana on the groups.

I have found that this overall vision is of paramount importance for the members of the small communities everywhere. Without it they are disoriented. Any serious study of the communities must consider the subject of the Church as communion and the Kingdom and its justice. It is a question of the groups wanting to see the context into which they fit. The Kingdom of God and its justice, the Church as communion and the small Christian communities are motifs in a great tapestry and we must pay attention to each without losing a sense of the total design.

NATURE OF THE KINGDOM

Even a cursory reading of the Gospels will show us that the Kingdom was the priority of Christ himself. It should still be the priority of his followers. Paul VI declares: "The Kingdom of God is to be considered as the absolute good so that everything else is subordinate to it."[27]

Jesus tells us that "the Kingdom of God is in the midst of

you" (Luke 17:21). It is that close. But what exactly is it? Jesus says many things about it yet gives no clear-cut definition. In Mark's Gospel Christ launches his mission in Galilee with a clarion call: "This is the time of fulfillment. The reign of God is at hand! Reform your lives and believe in the Gospel" (1:15). The Kingdom of God clearly means the rule of God. It is, as Langdon Gilkey puts it, "the concrete rule" of God in the world.[28]

Is it a real place? Gilkey thinks not. I feel, however, that this aspect ought not to be ruled out. Without discounting the spiritual aspect of the Kingdom, can we not, for example, look at a united human community in its geographical setting and say that the Kingdom of God is there? And doesn't the Book of Revelations remind us that in the end creation will be transformed into "a new heaven and a new earth" (21:1)? And that the one who sits upon the throne says, "Behold, I make all these things new" (21:5). So it looks as if there is a place in the *eschaton*, or eternal scheme of things, for this world of ours. Like the word of God and prayer, if the Kingdom is not made incarnate, does it not remain marooned on the island of ideas?

The Kingdom being the reign of God, we can say that wherever the graciousness of God breaks through to the world, there we find the Kingdom. Put another way, wherever there is genuine goodness, there is the Kingdom. "Grace" and the "presence of God" are alternative expressions for "Kingdom." I myself feel that one of the best forms of describing in what the Kingdom of God consists is to say that it is *harmony rooted in justice*. Certainly it is the description most relevant to the theme of this work. In other words, it is an effort to live out God's unchanging will for human beings, namely, that we be a community of brothers and sisters without divisions on grounds of race, color, so-called class, sex, age or whatever. That, surely, is the most refined expression of graciousness.

A profound harmony is, therefore, a vital element of God's reign. In this context there is a relevant story. One day a missionary put a question to a group of Indian children and told them that the first one to answer would be awarded a prize. All the dark heads clustered together for consultation. After some moments the children called out the answer together. Each of them had to be given a prize. It wasn't part of their culture to upstage one another.

That is the Kingdom: calling out the answer together.

The Kingdom is mirrored in the good Jesus. So it is that in John's Gospel the author does not speak of the Kingdom as a place or state; rather, it is attachment to the person of Christ. Thus instead of the familiar expression, "the kingdom of heaven is like" of the other Gospels, we get those "I am" statements: "I am the vine" (15:1–10); "I am the door of the sheep" (10:7,9); "I am the good shepherd" (10:11,14); "I am the way, the truth, and the life" (14:6). . . . In short, if we want to know what the Kingdom is like, we look to the mind, heart and values of Christ. This may explain a tendency in the Church to preach Christ and not to talk so much of the Kingdom directly, because in the figure of Jesus the Kingdom is made personal.

The Kingdom is openness. In my youth I once came upon a sorry sight as I reluctantly went to school. It was a hedgehog rolled into a tight ball. Around it lay the remains of a fire. Some wanton boys had apparently believed the story that if you lit a fire under a hedgehog that curled up for protection, it would simply uncurl and amble away. But the creature refused to open. Instead it closed up more tightly. And there it now lay singed and – dead.

If the Kingdom or for that matter the Church were to lose the quality of openness, its effectiveness would be severely curtailed. And if a marriage or family or community were to lose this quality, it would shrivel up and die as surely as that hedgehog.

Consider this dialogue:

JOHN: Teacher, we saw a man who was driving out demons in your name, and we told him to stop, because he doesn't belong to our group.

JESUS: Do not try to stop him, because no one who performs a miracle in my name will be able soon afterwards to say evil things about me. (Mark 9:38–39)

Jesus was nothing if not open and tolerant. And he did not favor weeding expeditions to get rid of all the undesirables (cf. Matthew 13:24–30).

The openness that characterizes the Kingdom was expressed in awesome fashion by Jean Donovan, Oscar Romero, Martin Luther King, Jerzy Popieluszko and Mahatma Gandhi. They lived and died for others. But a person doesn't necessarily have to die to make a heroic sacrifice. Mother Teresa of Calcutta tells of bringing a dish of rice to a desperately poor family in India. The mother of the family gratefully accepted the dish and immediately went and shared half with her next door neighbor.

Mostly, however, the outreach that marks the Kingdom is expressed in small ways that accumulate and are heroic only in their constancy: a smile, a hug, a humorous quip, a word of encouragement, tiny acts of significant sharing, attentiveness to the needs of others at table:

> little nameless unremembered acts
> of kindness and of love.[29] (Wordsworth)

Though the Kingdom is with us here on earth, it will not be fully realized until the hereafter. There is always a tension between the already and the not-yet (cf. 1 Corinthians 15:12–28). However, it is within the power of humans through their justice and compassion to make it more of a reality in the times in which they live.

A point regarding the Church and the Kingdom. The Church can be an exquisite expression of the Kingdom. It is part of the Kingdom. But it is not the whole of it. Wherever the graciousness of God breaks through to the world, wherever we encounter harmony rooted in justice, there is the Kingdom. It doesn't matter whether this goodness or harmony is found among Hindus, Muslims, Buddhists or Jews; we as Christians uphold and support it. At times the Church may not even be able to preach Christ directly, yet it can promote and give witness to his values which are worthwhile for all humans.

I'm not saying that we should not wish to attract people to Christ, whom we believe to be the key to our human destiny. Yet surely one of the best ways to draw folk to Christ is to have a Church that is open to the world in an effort to extend the reign of God. What we must not do is proselytize or force our point of view upon others. The Church does not exist for its own sake, but to express and promote the wider Kingdom. It is important for all of us to establish a clear identity. We Christians do so in the Church, and from there we reach out to all of creation.

In the course of this book the reader will have noticed that Christian community, when represented in diagram, is never depicted as a closed circle.

SMALL CHRISTIAN COMMUNITIES AND THE KINGDOM

Nowadays one of the special ways in which the reign of God is becoming evident is through the witness and outreach of the small Christian communities to the whole world. They are becoming increasingly effective as instruments to promote the Kingdom. Small communities within specific denominations are reaching out to the whole of creation but, more importantly, hands are joined across denominations as interdenominational groups strive to build the Kingdom together. One thinks readily of the Iona Community in Scotland or Corrymeela in Northern Ireland, but there are lesser known experiences in Ireland, England, the United States, South Africa and elsewhere. The consequent removal of religious barriers, quite apart from the outreach itself, is a striking sign of God's reign.

Interdenominational small Christian communities, precisely because they break molds in furthering the Kingdom, would surely be most dear to the heart of Christ. As death approached, his fervent prayer was "that they may be one ..." (John 17:11). But from experience I would respectfully make a couple of suggestions to persons contemplating the formation of such groups. Firstly, the members should be well grounded in their own particular beliefs, and there should be no attempts at proselytizing. Rather should there be respect for varying positions.

However, most denominations that call themselves Christian have much in common. They are family. The unique breakthrough of our era comes as Christians take steps to build unity and engage in common action with people of other religions—indeed with people who profess no religion at all. Thus are the Christian Churches becoming an integral part of world history.

A priest in Sierra Leone told me of a harvest thanksgiving ceremony that was held in a village there. The church was packed for the occasion, largely with Muslims. As the ceremony was drawing to a close, the muezzin in the tower of the neighboring mosque summoned Muslims to Friday prayer, yet the people waited respectfully until the Christian ceremony ended before going to the mosque. In the place of the Muslims, Christians would have acted likewise. These same people collaborated a great deal in their farming.

NOT JUST CHRISTIAN

The previous section was entitled *Small Communities and the Kingdom*. This recognizes the fact that persons coming together in groups to build a better world, or what Christians would call the Kingdom, is not confined to Christianity. The phenomenon is to be found among people of all creeds. Dom Helder Camara names such groups "Abrahamic minorities" after Abraham, the Jewish patriarch, because like him they are characterized by great faith, hope and generosity. Dom Helder says that these communities should be open to all but that the young have a special place.[30]

John Raines is more specific on the subject of these "Abrahamic minorities" in creeds other than Christian.[31] He tells us of a small community consisting of Buddhist monks and lay people in a village about one hour's drive from Bangkok, Thailand. It is called the Buddhist Development Community. For 30 years these people have led a highly active communal life and have spearheaded admirable work: building dams, fashioning an irrigation system, constructing dikes to keep back damaging seawater and improving the seed for their great cash crop, the sugar palm. And the program has been extended to other small villages.

This operation is not purely developmental. It grows out of Buddhist spirituality that has an enormous respect for the earth. The reverence for all of creation that characterizes their religion allows these Buddhists to become farmers in a way that is both effective and protective of the environment. They do not use insecticides or other chemicals, so the irrigation streams that bring fresh water to flourishing sugar palms and fertile gardens teem with fish. The result is that the villages encompassed by the program have an independent economy. And all this grew out of the activity of the Buddhist Development Community, comprised of monks and lay folk, motivated by a spirituality of great reverence for the environment. If we have ever thought—and some have—that Buddhism is life-denying, we must obviously think again.

Dr. Raines also tells of an experiment in Malaysia that does similar developmental work. It is named the Consumers' Association of Penang, or CAP for short. This, interestingly enough, is composed of Malay Muslims, Buddhist Chinese and Hindu Indians. The population of Malaysia consists of 50 percent Muslim Malays, 35 percent Buddhist Chinese and 11 percent Hindu Indians. The Chinese and Indians were brought in under British rule to do various kinds of work. CAP, though deeply involved with community life, is not ostensibly religious, nor is it motivated by reflections from sacred writings or any such dynamic. Nevertheless, the association is clearly wrestling with religious issues.

CAP is struggling against an idol—a blatant devotion to material things. There is a cultural invasion of the Third World, promoted largely by television programs produced in North America and Northern Europe. These programs incessantly urge people to buy a whole range of expensive and unnecessary products. In the face of this onslaught, CAP is desperately trying to preserve traditional spirituality, whether it be Muslim, Hindu or Buddhist. And traditional spirituality affords a place where people can stand and fight.

COMMON FACTORS

Given the spread of small communities that strive for a world that is more gentle, it is important that we look for points that they have in common. One trait noticeable in all of them is that they are *reaching out for the sacred*, though they give different names to this Ultimate Reality: Allah, Jahweh, God, Shiva, Love, Justice, Honesty or whatever. This yearning for what is holy *makes us all one* in a most important respect. And so we must ask ourselves some key questions. Is this Allah, Jahweh, God or Shiva to whom we all tend, in whom we are all one, happy with a world that is riddled with division and injustice? Must we not do all we can to confront injustice even to the extent of altering the structures of society that breed inequalities? Must we not work for a society where there is harmony rooted in justice and not simply a superficial harmony that papers over the cracks of all sorts of unfair practices? And since strength lies in unity, all the small communities that reach out for the sacred and work for a more sane society ought to build up an ecumenical network. In this way they would make their greatest impact.

The ecumenical aspect is noteworthy in the foregoing examples. Ecumenism in the end is a matter of ordinary people relating to one another in love. And I would suggest that this is best done through small communities. These can pray together and reflect on the word. Or like the Consumers' Association of Penang, they can join in action at the practical level. Practical, or Kingdom, needs are ecumenical. If a village requires a bridge, there is no such thing as a Muslim, Buddhist or Christian bridge. There are only ecumenical bridges that will equally sustain Muslims, Buddhists and Christians as they cross over a river in safety. Where relations between religions are concerned, theological discussion needs to be complemented with people at the grass roots *doing* ecumenism.

In conclusion we recall Paul VI's words: "The Kingdom is the absolute good to which everything else is subordinate." It is a mold-breaking statement. We recall too that small communities, Christian and other, are concrete expressions of that good and are instruments for creating it. And only when integrated into the vision of God's Kingdom with its justice do the small communities, and the Church itself, become truly intelligible.

SUMMARY

1. It is important for small Christian communities to have an overall vision of the context into which they fit—the Church as communion and the wider Kingdom.
2. The Kingdom of God is:

- the absolute good to which everything else is subordinate,
- the rule of God in the world,
- the graciousness of God breaking through to the earth ("grace" and "presence of God" are other names for the Kingdom),
- harmony rooted in justice,
- the person of Christ—his mind, heart, values, attitudes, and so on,
- openness and tolerance,
- already and not yet.

3. The Church can be an exquisite expression of the Kingdom but it is a part, not the whole, of the Kingdom. It too must be open.
4. Today one of the special ways in which the reign of God is becoming evident is through the witness and outreach of small communities, Christian and other. They are effective instruments for building a better world.
5. All creeds reach out for the sacred—a common element that should inspire us to work for a world where there is unity and justice and to form a network of small communities in order to do so.

4

Kingdom Justice

The word "justice" has cropped up continually in the foregoing pages. An increasing commitment to justice is also a feature of the Church emerging since Vatican II. It is, therefore, a concern of the small Christian communities and part of the integral vision to which they belong, a vision that they make concrete, or real, among us. If the direction of the communities is correct, they should as part of their development become involved in the justice issue. We must then understand the nature of this justice that is so important for the groups. The understanding is urgent in the light of Jesus' words:

> But seek first his kingdom *and his righteousness* [justice] and all these things shall be yours as well (italics mine). (Matthew 6:33)

And a similar urgency was conveyed by the Synod of Bishops in 1971:

> *Action* on behalf of justice and a participation in the transformation of the world fully appear to us as *a constitutive dimension* of preaching the Gospel, or, in other words, of the Church's mission for the redemption of the human race and its liberation from every oppressive situation (italics mine).[32]

In short we cannot truly preach the Gospel unless we act, and not just speak, on behalf of justice. The question, then, is not whether we should or should not *act* for justice, but, rather, what is the best strategy to adopt in the circumstances. It will prove helpful if we sharpen our notion of justice.

NATURE OF JUSTICE

Justice, according to the Bible and the documents of the Church, means having the following:

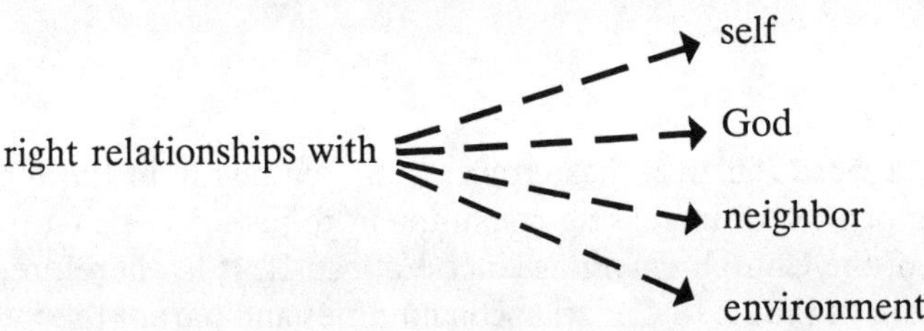

It is total in its approach to harmony. And isn't "right relationships" merely another way of saying "community" or "Kingdom"? These realities are all closely interwoven.

Oftentimes, when we speak of justice, we are thinking only of economic justice: fair returns for our work, proper conditions in working situations and so on. Justice, however, is much more than that because it touches all aspects of our existence.

I once heard a woman of African origin say at a meeting in a São Paulo *favela*, or poor district: "I am oppressed three times over. I'm oppressed because I am poor; I'm oppressed because I am a woman; and I'm oppressed because I am black." I was somewhat surprised to hear her say that she was oppressed because she was a woman. The men in the area, after all, were passionately involved in the issues of justice. And yet this woman and others, as it turned out, felt oppressed. So apparently the menfolk still lacked a clear understanding of the full nature of justice.

If relations between persons and, consequently, with God are marred by discrimination, justice suffers.

Respect for the environment is also part of justice. We have no right to strew the world with beer cans, discharge oil into our waterways or menace all life through leaks from nuclear power stations. The so-called Greens and those who protest against the bomb have an important message for us, namely, that the earth is the heritage not of one but of every generation. And we upset the delicate balance of nature at our peril.

A little poem called *Stupidity Street* by Ralph Hodgson[33] shows how the things of nature are so precariously linked together. The poem is all the more remarkable because it was written early in the century, when the public was certainly not as environment-conscious as it is today:

I saw with open eyes
  Singing birds sweet
Sold in the shops,
  For people to eat,
Sold in the shops of
  Stupidity Street.

I saw in a vision
  The worm in the wheat,
And in the shops nothing
  For people to eat;
Nothing for sale in
  Stupidity Street.

A final point regarding the foregoing diagram is necessary. It might seem presumptuous to put right relationships with self before right relationships with God. But the reasoning behind it is that, unless we can relate properly to ourselves in the first place, we are severely hindered in relating to God, neighbor or environment. The Kingdom, or reign of God, begins in our hearts.

A KINGDOM STANCE

The Church, and therefore the small Christian communities, must of course be involved in the struggle for justice. What is called for is something I might term a "Kingdom stance." All points of view and courses of action—whether social, economic, political or whatever—ought to be tested against our Kingdom stance or Christian principles. It is the Gospel and not a social theory, economic creed or political manifesto that has to be the mainspring of our lives. I am not first a sociologist, economist, or politician and then a Christian. First and foremost I ought to be a Christian.

A Kingdom stance means that in society I support whatever even remotely leads to harmony based on justice. There are those measures which quite obviously lead to this harmony, such as land reform or fair distribution of wealth. And there are others, famine relief for example, that could lead to this cohesion. It will only happen, however, if the people who give the relief realize in their reflections that they must take more radical action to get at the root causes of the problem. These causes have to do with structures and systems of sin that require "bold transformations and innovations that go deep."[34] A Kingdom stance challenges those good people to take a deeper look at the problems and opportunities. In other words it invites them to enter into a conscientizing, or action-reflection, process.

POLITICS

Since concern for justice touches all aspects of our existence, it naturally affects political life. During the Polish crisis of 1982 the Cardinal Archbishop of Cracow, while upholding the rights of workers, was accused by the military regime of meddling in politics. He defended his position and recalled that the same accusation was leveled at Archbishop Romero in El Salvador.

Politics is the active way in which our whole secular life is organized; it concerns itself with health, labor, sport, finance, education, industry and commerce, communications, welfare and so forth. That is why we have government ministries to look after these areas. Is the Church to have nothing to say in such matters? Must Christians busy themselves with incense and votive candles or retire to the sacristy? This is precisely what our opponents understand by keeping out of politics. Of course, this is absurd. We cannot opt out of politics, for to opt out of politics is to opt out of life.

In the course of my work I have come into contact with situations where people have suffered under either an extreme right-wing or an extreme left-wing regime. Both are equally abhorrent. Yet it is not uncommon to find persons with a one-eyed view of the world. Because they suffer, or have suffered under an extreme left-wing regime, they condemn it vehemently but are complacent about the evils of the extreme right. And vice versa. We should not allow ourselves to be used or fooled by either.

Whether someone is standing on your neck with a totalitarian right boot or a totalitarian left boot, the effect is equally excruciating. Yet, to survive, totalitarian regimes must have the unquestioning obedience of every last individual. Once there is even one solitary person who stands up and says "NO," the system begins to unravel.

The Christian must reach out towards *total freedom* and ultimately settle for nothing less. He will not rest content because his stomach is full if his voice is silenced. He does not have to look to Marx or to Adam Smith for inspiration. Rather does he look to Jesus Christ and measures the worth of all other ideologies against the words of Jesus. He does not live by the Communist Manifesto or the Capitalist Manifesto: he lives by the Nazareth Manifesto:

> The Spirit of the Lord is upon me,
> because he has anointed me to preach good news to
> the poor.
> He has sent me to proclaim release to the captives
> and recovering of sight to the blind,
> to set at liberty those who are oppressed,
> to proclaim the acceptable year of the Lord.
> (Luke 4:18–19)

SMALL CHRISTIAN COMMUNITIES AND POLITICS

What the small communities do exceptionally well is to prepare Christians to become acutely aware religiously, socially, politically and environmentally. They themselves are then quite capable of freely choosing the parties that most reflect Christian values.

On a recent visit to South America, I contacted groups with whom I had worked throughout the seventies. One of the things they have had to combat in the intervening years is persons trying to manipulate them for political ends. They have steadfastly refused to be drawn, insisting that the small Christian community is *a faith experience*, and not a political cell. Of course, their experience of faith in community does motivate them to make what seems in conscience to them the appropriate political option.

Good government (the type that a Christian could with a perfectly clear conscience support) would in the first place be deeply concerned with the weaker members of society: the sick, the mentally or physically handicapped, the homeless, widows and orphans, the old, the young, deserted spouses, single parents and so on. Having given priority to the weak, good government would then preoccupy itself with the happiness and well-being of the whole national family. Yet, while being concerned for all, it would not spoon-feed or be paternalistic to anyone; rather, would it foster self-reliance and self-respect in every person. And last, but by no means least, good government would promote a society where there is harmony rooted in justice and offensive inequalities are eliminated.

The Church has rightfully been critical of imperialism, colonialism, racism, sexism. . . . However, I feel that where a discriminatory classism is concerned, it has not been as vocal. For too long there has been an uncritical Christian acceptance of a totally unchristian class structure. Paul says: "There does not exist among you Jew or Greek, slave or freeman, male or female. All are one in Christ Jesus" (Galatians 3:28). Surely these words call for a classless society. So too, it seems to me, does Jesus' law of love. Yet even Christians readily fall in with the class system and use its terminology: upper, middle, and lower. How, indeed, dare we dub as "lower class" any person created by God? In so doing we are valuing folk not for what they are, but for what they have. True status comes from realities such as being human persons, children of God, brothers and sisters in Christ. And the nobility that matters is nobility of character. I think we might well take to heart the words of a Dublin teenager as she spoke of this problem: "It's high time we became aware of our blindness."

NEED FOR PROPHETIC WITNESS

In our world 40 million die of hunger or hunger-related diseases every year. This number is equal to the combined populations of Belgium, Canada and Australia. Every minute a figure fast approaching 2 million dollars (1.8) is spent on making arms. If a moratorium of two weeks was declared on the manufacture of lethal weapons and the money saved given to the needy, the basic food and health problems of the planet could be solved for a whole year. Can one imagine that in 1986, the United Nations International Year of Peace, 600 billion dollars' worth of weapons was produced? Surely an anomaly.

Furthermore, while one in every five persons in the developing world is underfed, one in every five in the major industrial countries is overweight or obese. So walking down the street in Boston can be quite a different experience from walking down the street in Calcutta.

And where children are concerned, a child in the so-called First World consumes ten times more than one in the Third. Which means that you would have to have a family of thirty in the Third World to consume as much as a family of three in the First.[35]

Everybody now lives with the menace of nuclear annihilation, the horror of chemical warfare and the awesome potential of even conventional weapons for destruction. We have even achieved the ultimate materialist obscenity in the neutron bomb, which destroys people while leaving buildings and property intact. Pope John Paul II recognized the dire state of things when he said at Coventry, England, on May 30, 1982:

> Today, the scale and horror of modern warfare—whether nuclear or not—makes it totally unacceptable as a means of settling differences between nations. War should belong to the tragic past, to history; it should find no place on humanity's agenda for the future.[36]

Only days later he went still further when he said in Argentina that all wars are "absurd and always unjust."[37]

It is a moot point whether a way of life that spawns horrendous weapons to preserve itself is worth preserving at all.

Millions of unborn babies are deprived of their most fundamental right: the right to life.

Old folk walk the streets of Dublin to keep their feet warm, others like them eke out their lives in isolation from their families in a senior citizens' home in New York. Ever-increasing numbers of homeless people sleep, wrapped in newspapers, under bridges in London. Little ones are discarded by their parents on the streets of many a city.

One day in Latin America I took up a newspaper and read a brief article that created something of a watershed in my own life regarding justice. It told of a young man who had collapsed and died on the street of acute anemia. Out of work, he had in desperation been selling his blood to the same blood bank so as to feed his wife and baby. There was a public outcry. The case was referred to the inevitable Presidential Commission where it no doubt languished and died.

Since Vatican II the Church has undoubtedly become more prophetic, or more concerned with justice. There is sore need for this, for a community that challenges all of us, governments included, to be just.

In being prophetic the Church is merely following in Christ's footsteps. The most outstandingly prophetic act in history was when he became flesh and dwelt among us. As Paul says: "though he was rich, yet for our sake he became poor, so that by his poverty you might become rich" (2 Corinthians 8:9). Rich, that is, in Gospel values.

OPTION FOR THE POOR

Jesus opted for poverty and the poor. The Latin American Bishops at Puebla (1979)[38] also made a preferential option for the poor and since then the whole Church has made the choice its own.

We say a "preferential" option for the poor because the Church doesn't slam the door on anyone. Neither did Christ.

When a wealthy person came to him, he invited that person to conversion, to an option for the poor and to a modest lifestyle. The rich young man sadly declined the invitation (Matthew 19:16-22) while Zaccheus with excessive generosity speedily accepted (Luke 19:1-10).

WHO ARE THE POOR?

If the Church is of the poor, then it becomes extremely important to understand who the poor are. Where does one who is educated and cultured (these too are riches) fit into the Church? Where does one fit in who is not lacking in worldly goods?

Puebla has done much fine thinking on the whole question of the poor. It really was a basic theme of the conference, as a glance at the index to the documents will reveal. It gives clear guidelines as to who the poor are.

Firstly the poor are the materially deprived, particularly those unfortunates who are so locked in a struggle for sheer survival, wondering where the next meal will come from, that they have no leisure time to devote to thoughts of spiritual or human enrichment.

The Hebrew terms for poverty used in the Old Testament (*ani* and *dal* in particular) convey a notion of powerlessness. So the poor are the "powerless" ones often bereft of even the will to fight or protest. The state of powerlessness, of course, usually accompanies material deprivation.

A friend of mine once landed at a certain airport. He handed his passport to the waiting official who put it in a drawer, carried on with the work he was doing, and ignored him.

After about five minutes my friend asked if he weren't going to return the passport.

"What passport?" enquired the official, feigning total ignorance.

To make a long story short, my friend eventually had to pay 15 dollars to get his own passport back.

Missionaries and voluntary workers are often harassed by imperious and corrupt officials like the one in our story. And appealing to a higher authority can be useless because the superior and the offender may be in collusion anyway. It is indeed a sobering taste of the powerlessness that is the lot of the great majority of the human race.

Included among the poor too are those who, though having sufficient worldly goods themselves, take up the cause of the poor and are one with them in their struggles. To have enough of the world's bounty is the right of every human being. There is no virtue in misery. Christ came to liberate us from misery. There is virtue, however, in a modest lifestyle: in living simply so that others may simply live. This is part of being a Christian, for we are followers of Christ whose lifestyle was simple in the extreme.

On various occasions I have met people who were at their wits' end as to how they might best break the apathy of what they called the middle-class Church. But there is no such thing as the middle-class Church. There is only the Church of the poor. So, if a priest were to find himself in a place where people are rather better off, he must urge them to live simply, to share their goods, and to be at one with the disadvantaged at home and abroad in all their strivings.

It is in this way that the well-off are saved. The Puebla option for the poor is not an option against the rich. The conference invites them to liberate themselves by liberating others.

APPROACHES TO THE PROBLEM OF POVERTY

There are various approaches to the problem of poverty. One provides straightforward *aid* to relieve human misery and deprivation. Sadly, it is only too often necessary. When people are starving, their immediate need is food, not a discourse on social justice. The difficulty about aid, however, is that if we give people something for nothing, we somehow lessen them as persons. In aiding folk, therefore, we must be creative in finding ways of preserving their dignity as human persons.

I knew a young lay missionary, John, who was rather good at this. The children of his area used to come to him regularly and say, "John, gimme ten pennies." John would then jokingly offer them a machete to cut some of the ever-flourishing grass that threatened to engulf his home. If they accepted, he afterwards paid them some well-earned money. And dignity was thus saved and self-reliance fostered.

Still another approach to the problem of poverty would be to promote the deprived through training, education and so forth. But we must try to avoid promoting people who go on to exploit others. Rather should we instill in them a strong sense of service and an appreciation of people above money.

Finally, when dealing with poverty, there is an overriding need for structural change. Society has to be reshaped. There must be "bold transformations and innovations that go deep" (Paul VI),[39] or as the Russian language succinctly puts it, *perestroika*.

Regarding justice, there is a statement by Tolstoy that the Church and every small Christian community would do well to ponder: "If once we admit," he says, "be it for a single hour or a single instance, that there can be anything more important than compassion for a fellow human being, then there is no crime against man that we cannot commit with an easy conscience."[40]

SUMMARY

1. Commitment to justice is a feature of the Church emerging since Vatican II.
2. It is therefore of concern to the small Christian communities and part of the integral vision to which they belong.
3. Justice consists in right relationships with self, God, neighbor and environment.
4. Respect for the environment is an important dimension of justice.
5. The Church and, consequently, the small Christian communities should adopt a "Kingdom stance" in their approach to justice.
6. A "Kingdom stance" is one that would support whatever leads to harmony rooted in justice.
7. It encourages a process of conscientization. This means that by alternating action and reflection we come to understand a problem-situation ever more fully.
8. Politics impinges on the justice issue.

9. Politics is the dynamic, or active, way in which our whole life is organized. The Church and, consequently, the small Christian communities must therefore deal with political matters.
10. The political extremes of left and right are equally abhorrent. The Christian should aim at balance and reach out for total freedom.
11. A small Christian community is *an experience of faith*, and not a political cell.
12. The small Christian communities so raise people's consciousness that they are well prepared to make political choices that are in harmony with their Christianity.
13. Good government is a matter of looking after the weaker elements of society, fostering self-reliance and self-respect, and promoting a society where there is harmony rooted in justice.

5

Experiences of Small Christian Communities—I

I have noted that one of the great learning moments in workshops about small Christian communities occurs when the participants are given the opportunity to study the stories of actual communities—and relate them to their own experiences. In the present chapter, I cite two such experiences from the industrialized world. They really speak for themselves. I chose them not because there is anything extraordinary about them, but because they are typical of so many other communities in other parts of the world.

As I set out to relate these stories—and those of the subsequent chapter—I should like to emphasize that the theological data given in the previous pages were largely distilled from these experiences and hundreds of others like them. And so too were the organizational guidelines found in the remainder of this work.

CRUMLIN, DUBLIN

The first experience I take from a big city parish in Dublin, Ireland. The area is composed largely of ordinary working people and in the current economic climate has more than its share of unemployment. The first member I interview is Ger Bailey (G.B.). His account is then complemented by that of Dolores Connell (D.C.).

J.O'H.: Ger, how did your group start?

G.B.: In 1982 there was a summer project for young people in the Crumlin parish. Father John Foster was in charge. Some of those involved in that successful project built up a camaraderie and felt they'd like to go on meeting as a group. They asked advice from a young Salesian seminarist who also worked on that venture. As you'll remember, he put them in contact with yourself and you spoke of the possibility of starting a small Christian community. Then, I understand, you helped them over a few months to get started. And so a group commenced meeting at the Salesian House in Crumlin. It was composed of some of those who had worked on the summer project and others who had helped on a Salesian work camp in County Limerick.

J.O'H.: Where did the experience go from there?

G.B.: Well, they met weekly and discussed topics such as "community," "justice," "problems of adolescence." . . . To tell the truth, they weren't too well up on these topics, but were aided by yourself and some Salesian seminarists from the Maynooth community. I believe you involved the seminarists because you had to go and work in Africa and didn't want to leave the fledgling community without help. Besides, the members were all on the youthful side.

J.O'H.: Yes, that's how it was and—

G.B.: But there's an important point—sorry, you were about to say?

J.O'H.: Please go on, Ger.

G.B.: There's the important point to make that in those early months those present had a sense that there was "something special" about their experience, that something important was happening. Anyway, the community gradually grew as some friends of existing members joined. It was at that stage that I myself joined. My wife, Gemma, who was then my girlfriend, was already a member.

J.O'H.: How about the organization of the community?

G.B.: During the first year we depended a lot on the Salesians as resource persons for our community. But fairly soon they started involving us in conducting parts of the meeting like discussions, Bible-sharing or whatever. They gave us a chance to use our talents and get to know each other. I suppose they were giving the opportunity for leaders to emerge. Eventually we felt the need to choose coordinators—that's what we called our leaders—and these were to come together and plan the meetings and activities of the group. We chose three. We felt that the coordinators could easily pick up the vibrations within the group and, by sharing and reflecting on them, help us on our collective journey.

J.O'H.: For how long do the coordinators serve?

G.B.: Some change takes place in the coordinating team annually, but we never change them all at the same time. So we have the advantage of new blood on the one hand, and continuity on the other. Also, with time, all use their talents in the service of the community.

J.O'H.: And decision making?

G.B.: We enter into dialogue, give and take, and come to a consensus.

J.O'H.: What sort of action, if any, did your community undertake?

G.B.: We were very conscious of the words of James about faith without works being dead and, consequently, about the need to *do* something. That was in the early stages. However, we were really beginning to know and trust one another. We began to think about the Kingdom and what it meant to us. We thought that, rather than take up a specific work as a community, we would try to share the sense of Church which we experienced in the small community with our families and friends. Our small community became a place of support, where we could share the experiences of our efforts to become more Christian.

J.O'H.: You shared your problems in the meetings?

G.B.: Many of the meetings were based on all we go through

in our lives: our worries, sadnesses, joys and achievements. Prayer too was becoming more important to us and we tried to look at our lives and bring Jesus and the Scriptures to bear on them more.

J.O'H.: So you complemented prayer with action.

G.B.: Yes. At the time, our members were becoming more involved in the wider parish community: scouts, folk groups, CAD (Community Against Drugs), Community Enterprise (to tackle unemployment), youth clubs, etc. We also tried to help another group of people start a community. This, however, did not prosper due to a fall off of interest on the part of that particular group; not a fall off of interest on our part, you understand. Again, there were some young people who had organized a summer project and wished to continue meeting (a repeat of our own experience), but sadly, the interest here also waned. We did help some folk to set up a small Christian community in Maynooth College, and this group still meets. The parish curates were contacted and invited to our meetings and we organized a successful youth Mass in the parish church. On more than one occasion members of the community have gone to address school audiences about our experience. Through reflection and prayer about our successes and our failures, we felt that we were constantly learning.

J.O'H.: Ger, would you like to tell us a little about the failures, the problems?

G.B.: No problem—

J.O'H.: That's great. You're really lucky.

G.B.: Wait a minute? I mean there's no problem in talking about problems.

J.O'H.: This is getting a bit like, who's on first base? Please go on, Ger. Don't mind me.

G.B.: In the time we have been together it has happened that people have joined the community and realized afterwards that it was not for them. Early on this did not affect us too much. With the passing of time, however, when this happens, we often feel a great sense of loss. Down the years some members have left the city altogether or gone to a different part of Dublin to study. One of our members went to Africa to do development work, but for his own good reasons did not rejoin us on his return. Another person left to become a Salesian sister. We miss them. However, many former members still visit us, when they are around, and it's always wonderful to see them.

J.O'H.: The pain of loss has been a problem, then?

G.B.: To lose a member is never easy. At one point a little group within the community was very unhappy, feeling they had been left behind by others. They thought the community was becoming too serious. During a very tense period we discussed this problem, but did not resolve it. Sadly, a few of the people who were unhappy left the community, feeling that they had been "driven out." At first this badly shook those of us who were left behind. But on reflection, we felt that our community was not what was needed by those who left. This experience, as with all our ups and downs (the lot of all groups), has been part of our formation. For us the proof that the Kingdom is thriving is the fact that, although smaller in number, the community is as enthusiastic as ever.

J.O'H.: Despite some disappointment you are still—

G.B.: Optimistic. The Eucharist has been a great support for us. It has been an important part of our community life and a great deal of preparation has gone into our monthly celebrations. If you have faith, you can't but be optimistic, can you? Some of us are also involved in the parish folk group, so we get to attend the same Eucharist on Sundays. There are many aspects to our community life apart from the weekly community meetings. We frequently go out together as a group socially and have even been on holidays together. Indeed, we once got marooned on a sandbank in the Shannon for a whole night. My faulty navigating was responsible, but I was amazed at how gently the group treated me, despite the gaffe. They would have been justified in making me walk the plank. Retreats and the visiting of other groups also make up a large part of our lives.

J.O'H.: You talk about the importance of the Eucharist for your group, but what about the word of God?

G.B.: It's odd you ask that, Jim. We have begun to feel that we don't bring the Scriptures into our lives enough. We think that we should now spend more time working with the Scriptures and trying to relate them to our lives.

J.O'H.: Anything else you'd like to add regarding your experience?

G.B.: About two years ago, I and another member, also called Ger, went to a week-long workshop on small Christian communities given by Father José Marins, a Brazilian priest, who has worked a lot with the communities. This experience proved most helpful. One member of our community is studying sociology and another theology. Another of our people is presently on a coordinating team for a youth resource center. The center is used for retreats and community prayer camps. Very recently Gemma and I brought together another group in our home. This is very important for both of us and we feel that it is a new stage in the development of the small Christian communities. We have also been in contact with other communities in Dublin and beyond. Not long ago we talked with a Scotsman, Ian Fraser, who with his late wife, Margaret, has done much good work in helping to build up a network of small Christian communities. And building a network is of the utmost importance for creating a sense of communion of communities. We are now in touch with a center in Scotland that, with others, is preparing for a European congress of small Christian communities in 1991. Much of the information on the communities is based on third world experiences, but our needs and difficulties are different. We are, however, learning all the time by sharing with other communities. All the foregoing are, I think, interesting developments.

J.O'H.: Indeed. And the future?

G.B.: As I said, through "networking" we would hope to make

the community of communities a reality. In our own parish we're lucky that the local clergy know us and are aware of what we are doing. We'd like, however, if the lines of communication were a little clearer sometimes. We hope that we can continue to help people on the road to community as a way of being truly "Church" as Jesus would have it.

(There follows the complementing interview with Dolores Connell.)

J.O'H.: Having heard Ger's account, Dolores, is there anything you'd like to say?

D.C.: Adding to what Ger has said about the beginning of our small Christian community, I think it is important to remember that it was a very slow process. We weren't at all sure as to what we were about . . . I mean most of the experiences we had heard of, or read about, were from the developing world. And we were in the industrialized world. We didn't have the same problems. As we read about the injustices in the developing world, we wondered what *we* could do . . . about those injustices . . . about injustices in Ireland. What action could we take. We did feel that we had faith, but, as Ger said, we realized that the Scriptures say faith without works is dead, so there was this urge to *do* something. Eventually we agreed with one another, and within ourselves, that living according to Christian values was what we should try to do. Maybe sharing with our families and in our places of work was just as important as going out and standing up for justice issues. . . . Nowadays we again feel a strong urge for even greater outreach, not least where matters of justice are concerned, but that's taken six years. We are slow coaches.

J.O'H.: A chief in Zambia once quoted a proverb of his people for me which says: "When God cooks, there is no smoke."

D.C.: That's nice. It's like in the Gospel when it says that, even when we are asleep, the seed of God's word is growing away silently. Maybe we people of the industrialized world are in too much of a hurry. We want things to happen yesterday. Time is God. . . . To continue: in the latter part of his account, Ger refers to problems with prayer and Scripture in our meetings. But we had those problems early on, as I remember. The difficulty was how to use prayer and Scripture in a meeting and preserve a balance . . . between prayer, Scripture and dialogue and decision making regarding relevant issues. . . . I mean, if we only had Scripture and prayer, we would be simply a prayer group and we didn't want that to happen. We wanted to be a community. We wanted–

J.O'H.: If I might interrupt for a moment. What do you see as the great difference between a prayer group and a small Christian community?

D.C.: It is a question of relationships. People can come together for prayer without necessarily relating deeply to one another. They are, therefore, not a community because what defines a community is the effort to relate at a deep level.

J.O'H.: Before I interrupted, you were saying how you wanted to balance the various elements in the meeting–Scripture, prayer, dialogue and so on.

D.C.: We certainly felt the Scriptures could help us in our everyday lives. At the same time, there was a lot we wanted to discuss. Getting the balance right has taken a long time.

J.O'H.: Does anything else present you with problems?

D.C.: For a while we were wondering what form leadership should take. Reading *Living Cells*[41] we became convinced that coordination/animation was the best form of leadership. Our community has a team of three coordinators and this works very well. Ger mentioned how we run matters on the basis of dialogue and consensus, but I must say it took us a long time to realize what this consensus was all about. We were so anxious to bring everyone along in our decisions that a small group held us back. A minority was in fact ruling. We didn't want majority rule, yet, in trying to avoid it, we actually fell into minority rule, so what we really had was minority rule and we thought we had consensus. Only in the last year or even six months have we come to grips with what consensus means. With consensus we have to agree even when we disagree. Am I making sense?

J.O'H.: There's a little touch of Irish bull about that last statement, Dolores, that people may find baffling.

D.C.: Let me try and take the bull by the horns, then! Very simply, we talk things over together until we settle upon something with which we all, or nearly all, agree. Then we act on that. Of course the decision is also informed by reflection on the Bible and prayer.

J.O'H.: What about the couple of members who are not in conformity?

D.C.: These make their feelings known very clearly. And it could be that they might change the mind of the community. But, if nearly all the community still want to move in a certain direction, they will see God's will in this and not stand in the way. Otherwise you get minority rule. Incidentally, Ger mentioned the problem of people leaving the community. That happened because of minority rule.

J.O'H.: How come?

D.C.: Well, a small minority were troubled by the idea of greater outreach and withdrew, because the others felt they could be held back no longer. Of those that remained there were still a few reluctant to get involved in greater outreach, but they nevertheless supported the decision and that was how the idea of a working consensus became a reality. . . . I don't know if Ger mentioned "process" and "formation." These were very important for us. We got a lot of guidance. After all we were virtually all only in our teens when the community started. Down the years the priests and seminarians that were our resource persons challenged us. Still we never felt that they told us what to do. When we decided to do something, it really came from ourselves. Making decisions for ourselves helped us to grow as a community in the past, when we were twenty members, and still does now that we are twelve. I would say that the resource persons were most sensitive and respectful toward the workings of the Spirit in the group. We are adults now, of course, and mature enough to run our own community. We still have clerical friends who visit us. Father Alan, a priest of our parish, was in recently and he was very interested and supportive. Then you join us when in Ireland.

J.O'H.: Purely to nourish my languishing faith, Dolores. If I might go back a bit. I'd imagine that the minority didn't systematically hinder consensus through dialogue.

D.C.: Not at all. Regarding most decisions, there was no problem at all. The difficulty was largely over the question of outreach.

J.O'H.: Any hard feelings towards those who felt they had to leave?

D.C.: None. Their going was painful to us. There's no denying it. Yet we're still friends, still in touch. In retrospect we realize where the root of the problem may have been. We had an influx of young members into the group at a certain point, but we had been going for some years at the time. The result was that in terms of process there were different levels in the community. When a bloc like that enters, it is better, perhaps, to encourage and help them to start their own group. About a year ago such a bloc presented itself and with help has started a small Christian community. It is going nicely.

J.O'H.: Regarding the first bloc who had difficulties over the question of outreach, did they all leave?

D.C.: No. Some managed to integrate themselves successfully into the community. Among those was one of our present coordinators. And incidentally, we've had individual newcomers who have also settled into the group. . . . However, we're still in touch with all former members of the community. Who knows, they may either return or become part of another small Christian community. A final thought regarding the group that left: a pity we didn't detect earlier that they were floundering because their needs, which were quite different from the rest of the group, were not being met. We might have been able to take successful action in time. We live and learn.

J.O'H.: In the course of our dialogue you mentioned the importance of "process" and "formation."

D.C.: Oh yes, I'm glad you reminded me. Well, it is crucial that we realize that Rome wasn't built in a day. Anything worthwhile that we do takes time, because humans need time to absorb things. . . . And, as a community, we have been eager to improve ourselves through courses—on the Bible, theology, organization and leadership, group dynamics, social teaching of the Church . . . and there have been retreats, workshops, lectures, meetings . . . sometimes, when we meet socially, we talk things over for hours and hours. And we have gone together to films, such as *Cry Freedom*, and discussed them at length afterwards. So you see, formation was important to us.

J.O'H.: From my knowledge of your community, I think you are shortchanging yourselves on the question of action. After all, from the very beginning there was hardly a constructive activity going on in the parish or area that one or other member was not involved in.

D.C.: It's true. The members were deeply involved in a whole bunch of activities: summer projects for children and teenagers, anti-drugs group, community enterprise group, group to fight unemployment . . . you name it. And yes, we probably did shortchange ourselves. But we were caught up in the idea that we should be out on the barricades standing up for justice. We didn't really see the things we were doing as action, because we did them even before the group started. It's as if you don't appreciate the gifts you have, because they are ordinary everyday gifts.

J.O'H.: Getting truly into justice issues takes time. It looks as though you have the awareness to get there now.

D.C.: I hope so. But then the whole country seems to be awakening to justice. The bishops, the Council of Major Religious Superiors, and various political groups are speaking out more and more about the plight of the poor. ... From films and workshops that we've had, we've seen that small Christian communities in Latin America and Africa are communities for sheer survival. They are tenaciously fighting for justice. Seeing their plight, I remember asking myself what we were doing or could do. And I thought that we must go for a simple lifestyle—not to expect to have a Porsche of our own or even the greatest house. Being thankful for what we've got and willing to share could be our way of being just to others. "Live simply so that others can simply live," as the Trocaire poster put it. This idea occurred to me in a workshop and stayed with me. Obviously, we couldn't do what the Latin American communities did. They're in the developing world while we are in the industrialized world. Sometimes I felt that we should all imitate what one member of our community, Leo, did and go as volunteers to Africa. We're still struggling with this whole business.

J.O'H.: Your community is now in its seventh year. What has kept you together for so long?

D.C.: That's a difficult one. ... Faith, I would say. No matter what changed in individuals or the community, we all still had faith in Jesus and in Christianity. We weren't always quite sure as to why we started, but we've really grown to believe in the whole idea of Christian community, and definitely believe it is the way forward. ... Sometimes we wonder if it's because we meet our friends that we go to community. It's great to see your friends all the time—to be part of such a friendly lot. However, there's the other side too. It's been awfully tough at times and we stuck it out. We respect each other's feelings. Then there are those moments when you unmistakably feel the Spirit moving in the community. It happened only last night in a new small community that our group is starting in the home of Ger and Gemma. When experiences like this occur, they are truly wonderful, keep you going ... make it all worthwhile.

J.O'H.: And where does your small Christian community go from here?

D.C.: We feel this urge to reach out. To establish more communities in our parish. There are a number of other discovery groups contacting us—wanting us to share our experience with them. This may be an outlet for setting up more communities. Then again as the members get older, we'll be getting married. Things will surely change for us. I hope, though, that we'll still be able to meet—maybe not so often—once a month perhaps. In this way we can bring Christian family back again. Also I'd like if we started small communities with our neighbors in our own homes. But the present members of our small community coming together in the future as Christian families is such an attractive idea. Maybe it's a pipe dream. I don't know.

J.O'H.: In many a place it's happened just as you envision it.

D.C.: Actually, four families from the Taize Prayer Group come together in our own parish to pray and talk about family life, so I don't see why it can't also happen for us. There's been a suggestion that we meet at Pentecost to discern our future. I think it's a lovely idea.

J.O'H.: Thank you, Dolores.

D.C.: Could I say one more thing that is close to my heart?

J.O'H.: Please.

D.C.: It's like a plea to the Church. As you know, we've had the heartbreak of seeing more and more of our young friends emigrate because of unemployment. Those of us who remain feel the terrible emptiness their departure leaves. Even from our own group we've lost Louise, Colm, Liz and Tim. But it is still more painful to see so many young people drifting away from the Church. They find it too hierarchical and institutional and can't participate. If only they could be helped to have an experience like we've had in our small Christian community, where there has been equality and total participation, the picture would be entirely different. Thousands . . . millions of youth would come alive in the cause of Christ all over the world. They say that Irish emigrants in bygone days were sustained by their faith . . . that Irish servant girls with their little contributions built St. Patrick's Cathedral in New York. But what will sustain those among the emigrants of today who set sail without any faith?

THE COMMUNITY OF ST. MARTIN–ST. PAUL/MINNEAPOLIS, MINNESOTA

Our second experience comes from the United States. What follows is an as yet unpublished interview with a member of the St. Martin Community, Mary Schram, conducted by Ian M. Fraser of the Basic Community Resource Centre, in Dunblane, Scotland. This is an *ecumenical* experience. The reader will notice how Mary found her way to the St. Martin Community by winding paths. Sometimes one experience of small Christian community leads to another. On occasions the demise of one group is merely the stepping stone to the birth of others. There are no success stories, or failure stories for that matter, where small Christian communities are concerned. There are only Gospel stories where honest effort and perseverance become the important elements.

I.M.F.: I believe you once belonged to another community, is that so? Could you tell us something about that one?

M.S.: I was a member of the Community of Christ, which was an ecumenical community that my husband and I started in Washington D.C. in 1965. He was called by the Board of American Mission of the Lutheran Church to start an experimental type ministry in the inner city of Washington D.C. We began that community with four adults and six children. In eight years it had only grown to seventy members. We lived under vows that we made to one another—for six months at a time, or a year. At the time, ministry was our main concern. We were very active in a lot of political activities. It was at the time of the Vietnam War and the Cambodian invasion by the United States government, the blacks' civil rights movement—all of that was going on in the inner cities. We were a worshiping community about one-third Roman Catholic, two-thirds Lutheran with a few other denominations scattered in.

I.M.F.: You said that you took on vows six months at a time. I suppose that means the vows changed. However, although they may have changed, the commitment, or dedication, must have continued.

M.S.: The commitments, or vows, didn't change; the length of time that we took them for changed. They included such things as promises to worship weekly in the community, to make a retreat at least once a year, to give up time and money, to be involved in a ministry within the neighborhood and to pray daily for each member of the community by name. Those were the five basic vows. We added some as the eight or nine years went on, but basically they remained the same.

I.M.F.: Was there any particular reason for leaving that community or were you just moved to something else?

M.S.: My husband was the Director of Lutheran Social Services of the Metropolitan Area and also pastor of the Community of Christ. I was working full time. Our four children were beginning to be in junior high and high school and the inner cities' school situation was beginning to concern us. We had purchased a farm in West Virginia with another family. We were concerned about the whole idea of nonviolence; wondered if it were simply a tactic that we had used during those years, acting against the Vietnam War etc., or whether that was the center of our faith. We wanted to get away from the city and just take some time and study the question that, as we say, rattled our cage. So we moved to West Virginia and lived there for six years on a farm, built a log cabin, and wrote a book on peacemaking and raised our children in that completely different atmosphere for a while.

I.M.F.: And then did you come to St. Paul?

M.S.: No, then we moved to Holden Village, which is a large retreat center on the Cascade Mountains in the State of Washington. My husband was called there to be director. That was another community that we lived in. It was not intended to be a community as was the Community of Christ, but it was something like that especially in the winter time—I would say that it was a community, because there were about 65 people that were snowbound for about nine months at a time! We had no television, no telephone. So we learned to worship and play and study together and create our own entertainment. It was again a worshiping community, that existed to host at least 5,000 or 6,000 people that went through Holden Village every year.

I.M.F.: Now at last you're in St. Paul/Minneapolis. How long have you been here? The community's been in existence for about two years?

M.S.: When we left Holden Village, we had discussed the possibility of—even intended—starting a community. There were volunteer staff at Holden Village who were interested in being part of a community that went on with the things we discussed at Holden Village; such things as peace issues, justice concerns, lifestyles, spirituality. . . . Many people felt that it was fine discussing such issues up in the Cascade Mountains of the State of Washington. But when they got back to "the real world," matters were not so easy. They felt they had no support base. So they were interested in being part of a community where these things were talked about. A community that had shared values. Not everyone in the congregations they normally attended shared their interests. Eight of these people lived in the St. Paul/Minneapolis area. So eight more of us agreed to move to St. Paul/Minneapolis to start what we were then calling the Community of St. Martin. There were about 14 or 15 who began the community in the fall of '84. We discovered that there were many other people who were also interested in those kind of values and those kind of justice and peace-making issues.

I.M.F.: I presume the community expanded then?

M.S.: Yes, it grew rather quickly. We now have about forty-two people who make a commitment to one another for four years at a time. The commitments are not specific, but each person tells the other forty-one members of the community how he or she will be accountable, and for what he or she will be responsible. Many of the commitment sheets talk about our worship life, our study life, how we will give financially. We promise to help one another, evoke one another's gifts, and help each other dream about ways of using our gifts in ministry in this neighborhood of the city. We ask specifically that all members say how they will do their peace-making. What each one will do personally, and what we shall do as a community. We are structured (this is our hope; it's not a complete reality yet) around small ministry groups. But not everybody in the community is associated with a specific ministry group, although they are all very much involved in ministry in their own vocation, in whatever they are choosing to do.

I.M.F.: What are the areas that these ministry groups work in?

M.S.: One is St. Martin's Table, of which I am a part. It is a peace education center in the form of a bookstore/restaurant. All those who serve are volunteers. There are about 50 people who give three or four hours a week; or they do that twice a month or as often as they can. All of the tips from the restaurant go to either a local, global, or national hunger project such as Food Shelter, Bread for the World, Oxfam, Catholic Charities or Lutheran World Relief. The educational part is not only the books and resources that we have which express the values of the Community of St. Martin—about 2,000 titles—but also on Friday nights we have forums on reconciliation issues. There is a discussion where maybe 50 to 80 people come and sit around tables and have coffee and cookies and talk about some reconciliation issue. It can be anything: from the present farm crisis in the U.S. to homosexuality—where there needs to be reconciliation between the gays and straights in the Church—the Philippines problem, South Africa, Central America, those kind of things. Then there is the Hospitality House that is going to open next month. It is a large three-story house. Three people plan to live in the place and host foreign students who come to the U.S. . . . students who have not had the chance to adjust to the culture. So they will be living there and donating any money that they can for their meals and for the space in which to live.

I.M.F.: From my experience in third-level education, I know how beneficial that apostolate is.

M.S.: Then we also have a very active Central American group that goes down to our senator's office every Tuesday and Thursday and speaks with the senator's staff about the situation in Central America. We write letters to them, read the letters out there and have a prayer vigil for fifteen minutes in the senator's office. Because of our consistency and nonviolence the senator has come to meet with us on two occasions, and we've had a couple of hours' visit with him on two occasions when he's been down in the cities. We did not have as much luck with our other senator, but we feel good about continuing to hold up the issue of Central America before our legislators. Then we have a project called Peace Partners. The community of St. Martin gives a stipend, room and board to two people who do peace work for the community. One is Jack Nelson-Pallmeyer who's just got back from two years' stay in Nicaragua. He has written several books, the last one *War Against the Poor: Low Intensity Conflict and Christian Faith* (Orbis, 1989). Jack is funded by us to teach. He goes around and lectures and brings before middle-class America the economic and political situation, especially in Central America. And the second person is a woman who is a part-time peace partner for us who simply works at St. Martin's Table, works with the hunger group, does things that are part of our peace-making activity. We give her a small stipend and provide her with room and board simply to help us in the peace-making efforts we're about.

I.M.F.: There is a kind of spirituality that is the aim and the basis of the community, is that right?

M.S.: Everyone has a center to his or her spirituality. Some people have what we would call a pietistic center. I think Lutherans have a doctrinal center of spirituality. Yes, we're talking about a center. Without saying that this is the only center for our spirituality, the Community of St. Martin is trying, as far as their personal growth is concerned, to live by a nonviolent, justice-centered spirituality. My definition of spirituality is how you live out your life, how you view things. If you see things from a pietistic center, that will be how you live out your life. If you see them from a doctrinal center, that will be very important to you. If you live life from a justice center or a nonviolent center of spirituality, that will affect how you see things, how you view enemies, those you dislike. So a nonviolent spirituality is what we would say we hope is the center of the spirituality of the people and the Community of St. Martin.

I.M.F.: Is this community your church instead of a normal parish church?

M.S.: Unlike the first community I was associated with in Washington D.C., where we were a congregation of the American Lutheran Church (at least the Lutherans in the community formed a congregation), the Community of St. Martin is different. We are all members of local parishes, whether they are Roman Catholic or Lutheran. We come together because of a common interest in peace and justice issues and for our worship life. We have five opportunities to worship a week, but it's not on Sunday morning, or the regular time for worship in our own congregations. We had hoped that being members of the community would make us be a leaven and light in a congregation. What we're finding is the community demands so much of our time that we are not able to put into our congregational life the kind of commitment that we had hoped. We're still working on that problem. It's a difficult problem, I think, that we face.

6

Experiences of Small Christian Communities – II

There follow two experiences of small Christian communities from the Third World: one from Latin America and one from Africa. Again they are chosen not because they are special, but because they are fairly typical. I realize, of course, that small Christian communities are molded by, and respond to, local circumstances and therefore differ greatly not only from one country to another, but even from one area to another. Nevertheless, having experienced the groups widely, I find that they have much in common around the world, and much to say to each other. Like the Gospel itself, they deeply penetrate the cultures in which they are received – affirming what is good, challenging what is not.

LA COLMENA, QUITO, ECUADOR

(This is certainly an experience where the influence of place and circumstance, impinging on the life of a small Christian community, becomes clearly apparent. For here is a group which is part of a society and Church that are, historically, at the cutting edge of events. I am recalling this story from personal recollections and notes made at the time.)

It all began with courses at the parish center in 1972. There were classes in electrical installation, photography, dressmaking, cooking and hygiene, first aid, music and languages. It was rather as if a people's college existed, although we only had the use of one hall and volunteer teachers. Widespread unemployment in the *barrio* was a factor, and many of the participants in the courses were hoping to acquire skills that would enable them to earn a living.

On the pastoral side, every Thursday evening was given over to conferences and open discussion on requested topics: drugs, alcoholism, violence to achieve political ends, active nonviolence, love and sexuality. . . . These were well attended, especially by young people.

A youth Mass was also started. It was not that adults were excluded, but, if they came, they knew the celebration would have a youthful flavor. At first the Mass was held on Sunday mornings and for one year continued so. The numbers were steady, but not large. At the suggestion of the young people themselves, the celebration was eventually transferred to 6 P.M., a more suitable time, and flourished. Some only found standing room. Most of the young Christians who attended were at state schools, where no religious education was given. So, using the events of the liturgical year, an effort was made to make a substantial point in the homily each week, in order to build up religious knowledge and personal commitment. Indeed this Mass continues to the present day and has been extended to other parishes of the archdiocese.

A Small Christian Community Emerges

From all the foregoing there emerged seven young men who proposed that meetings be held to reflect on the Scripture and for planning activities to help their *barrio*. All were male to begin with, but the anomaly was noted and quickly remedied. Soon they were joined by females.

There had already existed in the area a group of young people that was something of a think tank on social issues. They had offered to join the discussions going on at the parish center, "provided religion was not mentioned." They were honestly told that this would not be possible, and came nonetheless. Some members from this group were to form the backbone of the emerging Christian community, and, indeed, its leader is now an ordained priest. I think that what impressed them was that in the parish center, not only was there discussion, but there was also action. And then they did have a sneaking regard for Christ. It is hard to ignore someone who hangs on a cross for his principles.

The newly founded small Christian community grew quickly and within no time there were two groups. Other groups were to start around the neighborhoods and continued for a time, yet faded. It was a case of the original groups trying to spread their wings too soon before they had firmly established their own identity.

But let us follow the fortunes of the first group. The word of God was important to the members and they quickly related it to their own lives with their problems/opportunities. I have always found Latin Americans rather good at doing this. Slowly and, one must admit, with lapses in commitment the community began to *do* things: to help with the religious education of children, to run a children's club and to organize summer camps for children and youth....

A Pastoral Plan

The group grew in commitment and consistency and became even more serious about its plan of action. Consequently, after a couple of years it did a thorough socio-pastoral analysis of its area, an analysis that took some months to do. As a result, three generative problems were unearthed, three problems that generated many others. These were grinding poverty, lack of educational opportunities and disunity.

The small community then decided to focus its efforts and resources, such as they were, on these particular problems. As one can imagine, its economic resources were scarce. Apart from the area being poor, the members were mostly youthful. What they did have to give they gave generously and with goodwill—service. And every effort that they made was directed at one or another of the generative problems. Examples of their endeavors were a night school for preliterate people on the premises of a sisters' school, technical courses, conferences and discussions, youth Mass, youth Easter, a district magazine, summer camp, youth clubs, religious education, a crafts center....

It seemed the time was also right for the communities of La Colmena to spread their wings. (You will remember that a second community soon followed the first whose story we are recounting.) Accordingly, groups were started in two other areas: La Ferroviaria and Athualpa.

Given the injustices that prevail in Latin American society, the communities of La Colmena, and also those of La Ferroviaria and Athualpa, through action and reflection, got involved with the whole justice issue.

MAY DAY, 1978

The preoccupation crystallized on May Day of 1978. The communities decided to march in solidarity with the workers, but as a Christian group with suitably Christian slogans. The banner at the head of the communities, for example, declared in the words of Paul VI: "The new name for peace is justice." Among a plethora of noisy groups, they participated as one that favored active nonviolence in the tradition of Mahatma Gandhi. In the midst of all the noise, they also decided to walk in silence—something that caused them to be the focus of much attention.

Eventually the demonstration, instead of flowing along, ended in a hostile flood of people roaring defiance in front of the Presidential Palace. The police intervened. Panic spread. People fled in all directions. The Christian group, however, held fast and commenced walking back to base in an orderly fashion.

Soon, about 100 yards ahead, they saw a line of soldiers with rifles ready, barring their path. The communities steadily advanced in silence. There was neither the customary yelling of abuse or stone throwing. The soldiers were completely baffled. Active nonviolence and silence they did not seem able to handle. Like the waters of the Red Sea, then, they miraculously parted and allowed the group to pass through.

But that was not the end. At the next corner an armored car with powerful water cannon was perched in waiting. Tension mounted as the participants confidently expected to be bowled over and dyed for future identification by powerful jetties of liquid from the cannon. Still, they advanced silently and steadfastly. The armored car roared as it revved up its powerful engines. Then it moved away to let the group pass.

The communities had gone forth in the morning fortified by prayer and the word of God: "... make a defense to anyone who calls you to account for the hope that is in you ..." (1 Peter 3:13–18). They returned home having been deeply impressed by the eloquence of silence and the power of active nonviolence, and love. The whole episode has remained in the memories of the communities as something of an Exodus experience.

PROBLEMS/OPPORTUNITIES

Following the exhilaration of the biblical Exodus, the Jews ran into great difficulties. So maybe this is the place to speak of the problems that the community in La Colmena encountered. Since the group was largely composed of young people, emotional problems were among the first to arise. Romance blossomed between certain persons in the group and there was the danger that they would become too absorbed in one another, cutting themselves off from the other members. Yet problems are not simply problems; they are also opportunities for growth. The difficulty was met head on and discussed by the community. If someone found romantic love or a good personal friendship within the group, all agreed that this was a good thing. Nevertheless, the persons concerned would have to take care not to be exclusive within the community, but give due attention to all. It should be remembered also that the members came to the group primarily in search of Christ. In short, a small Christian community has always to balance respect for the needs of the person with respect for the needs of the group.

The second problem proved more intractable. It had to do with evaluation. Since the community was composed of young people, they needed the help of an adult. I was the first to fulfill the role of adult resource person. I tried to befriend and guide the members, but without imposing my views upon them. Looking back now, however, I feel that at times I may have done too much for them.

An example may help. When the groups chose their own coordinators, these leaders were naturally supposed to run the meetings. Sometimes they would arrive without anything prepared, and, rather than let everything collapse, I would step in and conduct the session. Perhaps it would have been more salutary to allow the meetings to flop and the coordinators to flounder. That way they would have become more independent.

When I left, the adult resource persons who followed seem to have been more "hands on" folk. That did not work either. Then, rightly or wrongly, various people also felt that some members were relied upon more than others. The result was friction and frustration for all concerned; eventually, the group found itself without adult guidance for two years. In retrospect, the members realize that their own immaturity contributed to the impasse and are grateful to those hard-pressed adult helpers for the patience shown. Though left alone, the community survived.

Although I had been with the group in La Colmena for the best part of a decade, they felt that I had gone too soon. That may have been so. In the light of later experience, however, I think the weakness may have been in not helping them to shoulder responsibility and develop autonomy sooner. Some groups that I have been associated with since did this in much less time and with much less assistance.

I returned to La Colmena in the summer of 1988 after ten years and found the original community still in existence, though the members had all changed. "That we are still in existence, despite the difficulties we have encountered, is proof that the Holy Spirit is great," said Pablo, one of the present coordinators of the community. I remembered Pablo well. When I first met him, he was a little boy participating in the first summer camp run by the original group. "Those camps made us so happy," explained Janette, wife of Pablo and another coordinator, "that we wanted to do the same for the children of today." Which explains how I happened upon them running a summer camp. The experience was moving. As I looked at this modern-day Priscilla and Aquila, I could only marvel how the work of the Spirit endures, despite our poor human blundering. There is never any reason for us to feel alone in our apostolic endeavors.

And what of the members of the original community? They are married now, for the most part, and spread throughout the city of Quito. Though from a working people's area (*barrio pop-*

ular), nearly all of them struggled to get a university education and now have professions. But they have not forgotten their roots. Alberto, Fabian and Vicente, lawyers, have a Rescue Foundation and give free legal aid to prisoners who cannot afford it, and they have also organized an education program with certification in a major prison. Mario, Narcisa and René are medical doctors who give their services free, or at greatly reduced rates, to the poor. Pablo is a teacher who instructs preliterate people, Pepe and Pedro work with youth groups, Janette gives religious education, and so it goes. When I met them in the summer of 1988, they had begun to come together again and were determined to meet at least once every three months. They were also determined to get involved in the communities where they now found themselves.

All of them are grateful to the group for the excellent formation, sense of awareness and incentive that it gave them. That the membership of a community should change with the years, or that it cease to exist as such, is not the issue (it may be an inevitable part of a life process). What is important is that the spirit of the original small Christian community should live on in other new communities.

The group of La Ferroviaria is now stronger and more cohesive than even the parent group of La Colmena. The original members of the group, unlike those of La Colmena, stayed within their own district. They do much good. Most are now married and form exemplary families, which give each other a great deal of support. The Athualpa small Christian community also continues.

ST. MARTIN'S PARISH, FREETOWN, SIERRA LEONE

Here we are dealing with about a dozen small Christian communities pioneered by two young Spiritan priests, David Kennelly and Noel Kilgarriff, who have worked closely with their people. What I have noticed is that many of the problems that beset small Christian communities in Africa, and indeed elsewhere, are quietly worked through by two pastorally sensitive and tolerant priests and their responsive parishioners. Examples of these problems would be the following:

- relating the small Christian communities to existing associations, the parish council and the pastors,
- reconciling tradition and change,
- involving youth and women,
- moving from prayer and the word of God to action,
- getting people to share with rather than lecture one another,
- motivating members to enrich themselves spiritually, intellectually and humanly,
- overcoming the aches and pains of leadership.

Noel Kilgarriff kindly gave the following interview. Indeed, the recording is enlivened by the sounds of Africa in the background, among them a bird singing lustily.

J.O'H.: Would you like to say first of all, Noel, how you got started?

N.K.: St. Martin's was established as a new parish in 1953. In 1983 it was divided in two. One parish still retained the name St. Martin's, while the other was called Holy Cross. Father David Kennelly and I, two young priests, were asked to come to St. Martin's. David had been involved a great deal in encouraging small Christian communities there. The general chapter of our order in 1983 also animated Spiritans to foster the small Christian communities. When David and I arrived at St. Martin's in December 1983, therefore, it seemed the thing to do. We held a seminar in January–February 1984, inviting as many as we could. Actually, 24 came from St. Martin's and 12 from the neighboring parish of Holy Cross—the previous pastor of St. Martin's, Father Paddy Moore, had done much to encourage lay participation in the parish and lay leadership out in the neighborhoods. About that time you were in Sierra Leone sharing on small Christian communities and gave us a push in Freetown as well.

J.O'H.: Yes, I remember the enthusiasm and sense of expectation of the lay leaders.

N.K.: That seminar dealt with summaries of passages from the Acts of the Apostles which treated of the early Christian community—what it looked like. It examined the notion of community in the Trinity, or in God. And we asked ourselves if, based on our own experience, we couldn't imitate in our parish the small communities that we read about in the Acts. Admittedly, in our own communities there were aspects similar to the groups in the Acts, yet some things were missing. The idea of going back into our homes to pray and form small communities was attractive to people. Anyway, they decided they'd try and we split into two groups of twelve – one on the right of the parish and one on the left. The members of each group worked together for a year, praying every week, following the Seven-Step Method for studying the Bible put out by the Lumko Institute in South Africa. Eventually, they began to break up and form other cells. These cells had their ups and downs: at the moment we have 12 small Christian communities in the parish.

J.O'H.: So that's how you got started.

N.K.: Yes, that's about it.

J.O'H.: Where have you gone from there? Could we hear something of the ups –

N.K.: And downs? The first few years were geared to setting up and spreading the communities. That was the major task. And going from two groups to nine was an important step. There were lots of difficulties involved in this. We priests were already greatly overworked and here we were bringing in another priority for the parish. We really saw the establishment of small Christian communities as the priority, yet we were totally bogged down in traditional parish – and other – activities. Then there were the tensions in the parish community; tension, for example, between those involved in the longstanding associations and the members of the newly formed small Christian communities. It took quite a while to work through that tension.

J.O'H.: It will be interesting to hear how you did that. The relationship between the emerging small Christian communities and the established associations is an important issue on the African pastoral scene.

N.K.: The problem was that those who were members of the parish council and various associations, such as the St. Vincent de Paul Society or Catholic Women, were few in number. We were talking really of about 30 parishioners, and the same people were overlapping in a lot of parish associations. It was a status thing. Some people felt that the more feathers you had in your cap, the more organizations you belonged to, the better parishioner you were. They were going to many meetings and representing the parish in other places. So it was a cozy little club.

J.O'H.: And the remaining parishioners?

N.K.: I'm coming to that. . . . Those 30 people were deeply committed. I don't deny it. It was just that we were encouraging the active involvement of more and more parishioners. We had done a census and discovered that there were about 3,000 Catholics in the parish. Of these, 30—well, let's say 100—were actively involved. The question was how to interest the other 2,900 in the life of the parish.

J.O'H.: A good point.

N.K.: This is what the small communities were trying to do. Some of the parish councilors and members of the associations took part in the small Christian communities, others didn't; those who took part were for them, those who didn't felt the associations were going to die. They felt threatened. Gradually, we tried to have workshops where people could talk about the problem and express their feelings.

J.O'H.: That was an excellent idea.

N.K.: We were trying to get the associations to work with the communities. To convince the youth, for example, to form a youth dimension within the small Christian communities, the women a women's dimension. Again, so that the task of relieving material want would not be left entirely to them, we encouraged the members of the St. Vincent de Paul Society to get the groups to look after the needy. We didn't want special needs being left entirely to just a few people.

J.O'H.: Is it the idea that every small Christian community ought to be a justice and peace group, a St. Vincent de Paul group or whatever?

N.K.: Exactly. . . . The youth group and the women's group did get more involved with the small communities. Nevertheless, the tensions persisted. The St. Vincent de Paul Society, for example, might have a meeting on a Monday and so too might one or other small Christian community. The trouble was that these organizations had members in common. So the question arose as to where those members would go. Where we priests were concerned, there was the same issue. The St. Vincent de Paul people expected us to attend their weekly meeting, yet we felt we would also like to go out to the small Christian communities. Gradually, then, we withdrew from the associations somewhat, and they began to understand that we had to go out to the neighborhood groups. If we turned up in the associations once in every three or four meetings, they were happy.

J.O'H.: Have the associations come to accept the small Christian communities now?

N.K.: I think so. For the first two years, the small communities were developing out in their own areas away from the parish center and there was little reference made to them. Their meetings were announced in church and we preached on the subject of the groups sometimes, but that was all. They never came together or figured in the parish church until 1987. During the rains that year, we, the priests, weren't able to get to the groups, and it was left to a catechist, who was really enthusiastic about small Christian communities, to animate them. Not only did they survive during the rains, when we weren't around, but they became quite well coordinated.

J.O'H.: Did that help their self-confidence?

N.K.: So much so that they decided they'd have a Mass of thanksgiving in the parish church. There was also the incentive that they were three years in existence. They got together then to plan the liturgy. Some coordinators, representing the various small communities, held meetings and then reported back to their groups. The communities had a gathering where they sang a number of hymns and chose the ones they liked best for the liturgy. A few members circulated among the groups afterwards to make sure the hymns were practiced. So there was much intermingling, which was new for them. And the small Christian communities discovered from this activity that they were much stronger than they realized.

J.O'H.: How did the ceremony go?

N.K.: It was, as they say, massive. A procession of members entered from without and came up the center aisle of the church. The parishioners who didn't belong to the communities were in the church waiting for the Mass to start. Suddenly you had these 150 people burst into the church singing. It really took those present by storm, I think. Many of them joined the communities after. They didn't know that they were so strong and so positive. They sensed a new vitality. And during the liturgy local languages and local musical instruments were used for the first time—a tremendous breakthrough for Freetown.

J.O'H.: It goes to show that the living witness of small Christian community is more powerful than a million words used to describe it.

N.K.: Just so.

J.O'H.: And they used the vernacular and local instruments—that's interesting. Freetown tends to be conservative, doesn't it?

N.K.: Very. It looks to the West . . . to the traditional Anglican Church. Innovation is a problem. The young people were the only ones who tried to alter standard approaches to liturgy, but they were looked upon as mavericks. Here, however, was a group of adult Catholics—parish councilors, association members—really taking on a new thing. The result was that those parish councilors and association members who were against the small Christian communities, felt threatened by them, began to see them in a new light.

J.O'H.: They have accepted them?

N.K.: Yes, some have asked to have small Christian communities in their homes; some have become real leaders in this new apostolate. Furthermore, the small communities now have representation on the parish council and have brought a new dynamism to it.

J.O'H.: I have a feeling, Noel, that the points you are making are going to be enormously helpful to other small Christian communities, especially in Africa.

N.K.: Please God our experience may be helpful to someone. . . . That was how matters stood in 1987. Since then, the groups have truly blossomed. Each community chooses its own coordinator and all the coordinators combine to make a coordinating body.

J.O'H.: Is this coordinating body different from the parish council?

N.K.: It is. . . . Up to now each small Christian community has sent a representative to the parish council, but that representative didn't have to be a coordinator, or leader, of a small Christian community. Elections for the parish council are due soon, and they will have to review the whole question. The idea of coordinators for the groups came up, as you will remember, to answer liturgical requirements in the first place. However, they have continued and the combined coordinators now meet every two weeks in the church compound. The purpose of course is to network and, where necessary, coordinate activities. To further achieve this, the combined coordinators have introduced a general meeting for all small Christian communities once a month.

J.O'H.: A communion of communities?

N.K.: That's it. And they built a palaver-hut big enough to allow people to sit round in a circle and talk.

J.O'H.: Now that you've touched on the matter, would you like to say what action, or apostolate, your communities are engaged in?

N.K.: At the beginning they were very much into the prayer-meeting and very little into action. But, then, members in the same street realized that they were fellow parishioners and began to reach out to one another. They made small collections to help with funerals and school fees. An old person in the area might need help.

J.O'H.: Somebody ill . . . ?

N.K.: Cases like that. They helped. Not just their own members or fellow Christians, but also other needy people in the neighborhood. The body of coordinators, which was more oriented towards the neighborhoods than the parish center, got the members of the small Christian communities to focus on the needs of their own areas. It might be a question of getting good drinking water. . . . One group decided they were going to repair the roads and are now getting round to it after the rains. The coordinators asked all the small communities to examine the needs of the parish and they came up with the idea of a nursery school as an urgent requirement.

J.O'H.: Why was that?

N.K.: One has to be six here before being accepted for primary school; consequently, many children were hanging around the streets, missing an opportunity to learn. Both parents had to work to make ends meet. We spent much time discussing whether it really was a general need or simply the need of a few. Actually, the need was great. We set up a school in the parish hall and it now has over 300 children. It's a success. The communities saw this as their own project, which was wonderful. Then, as a result of this endeavor, the parish built toilets and a playground for the nursery. The whole area was insufficiently developed, however, so the groups decided they would build a stage and extend the playground. That whole space could then be used for parish functions and fund-raising ventures. Every weekend 40 or 50 members came and supplied the labor, while the parish provided the materials. Womenfolk did the cooking. The common project engendered a great sense of community.

J.O'H.: Common projects are especially good for building community, aren't they?

N.K.: Indeed. The only fear we had was that, like in the old days, everything would become centralized in the parish compound. Celebrations and erecting buildings at the center were only means of fostering the spirit of community. The real hope, however, was that there would be development back among the small Christian communities. This is now happening: one group is making soap, another headgear, a third is collecting firewood and selling it. . . .

J.O'H.: Action, then, there certainly is. Perhaps at this stage you'd like to say something about the meetings of the small Christian communities?

N.K.: Father David is a great resource person for the Bible. And he introduced the groups to the Seven-Step Method put out by the Lumko Institute in South Africa [something along the lines of the method given in Appendix 1]. He found it a useful technique to get groups started and it's easy to learn. It was a problem to stop people lecturing one another, which the Seven-Step Method discourages; and it was also difficult to prevent the meetings from becoming purely talk shops without any resultant action, which the method equally discourages. By continually drawing attention to correct procedures, these flaws were ironed out. David did not confine himself to this method, however. He used other approaches; not least among these was starting with a life problem and then seeking light from the Bible as to how it might be solved. But the great thing was that ordinary Christians were being encouraged to read the Bible—something that was happening the world over. At the time, also, the Seven-Step Method was being adopted nationally, so what we were doing locally fitted into that endeavor.

J.O'H.: There was a pastoral team functioning at the national level?

N.K.: Yes. They encouraged the Seven-Step Method, for example, and also fostered the DELTA program (Development, Education and Leadership Training in Action).

J.O'H.: Could you elaborate on the DELTA program?

N.K.: It is an integral program that deals with the subjects of development, education and justice awareness, but doesn't stop at theory. It trains leaders, giving them the skills to go out and motivate others to deal successfully with problems through reflection and effective action. The leaders the program prepares are nondirective, which means that they get people to think, decide and act for themselves. Some of the younger coordinators of the small Christian communities who weren't tied down by family commitments did the DELTA training course. With them was our catechist, Martin George, who had also done a youth course at the Kenema Pastoral Center and a further study on groups and cooperatives in Nigeria. He was quite familiar with the dynamics of small Christian communities and was a great help. Anyway, these young coordinators came back from their DELTA course and shared what they had learned with those leaders who found it impossible to get away. This sharing provided the motivation for the action that we have already seen. One of the positive aspects of DELTA was that the leaders had to plan for six months and evaluate when the six months had passed. This helped to get all our leaders and people into an action-reflection dynamic that proves beneficial. It prevents them from stagnating or going about their tasks unthinkingly. A second DELTA team was trained to lighten the burdens of the first. Previously, David and I took a big hand in organizing and giving courses in the parish and even in the whole city of Freetown. Nowadays this is largely in the hands of the DELTA teams. So David and myself—the two priests—have taken a back seat. We attend meetings now and again. We sit in at the coordinators' session, but we don't really lead now. Much growth has taken place in the small Christian communities.

J.O'H.: I understand that the Chinese use two characters to describe the word "problem": the first means "crisis" and the second "opportunity." So every problem is not simply a problem but also an invitation towards progress. Any other problems/opportunities you would like to touch upon?

N.K.: The situation of the youth and women. The women were quiet in the meetings; they let the men do all the talking. Anyway, that's what happens in traditional society and, even in the Muslim culture (we have many Muslims here), the women sit outside the mosques or on the edge of the gatherings. We tried to get the coordinators of the small communities to involve the women in leading discussion. This helped, and there was a curious phenomenon. Wherever David or I went to the small Christian communities, we attracted men. On the contrary, wherever Sister Therese, a pastoral worker in our parish, went, she attracted women. We ended up, then, having one or two groups completely composed of women, while the remainder were composed of men, even though the groups supposedly represented an area. We decided we'd have to move around. Therese started visiting the men's groups to attract women and we visited the women's groups to attract men. Do you follow me?

J.O'H.: I'm struggling. . . .

N.K.: Eventually it worked itself out, though some of the groups still have a predominance of either male or female.

J.O'H.: And the youth?

N.K.: The young people felt somewhat threatened by the small Christian communities. They were already in difficulty with the elders. It was the generation gap. They felt they had no say in matters affecting them. We did encourage the youth to take part in the groups, yet without success. We decided, then, not to push too hard and took a low-key approach. In practice they did get involved over the years. One group is in an area where there is a concentration of young people and these tend to figure a great deal in that group. From the vantage point of the group, the youth wrote songs for, and introduced local instruments into, the liturgical celebrations of all the small Christian communities. The group the youth were involved with, therefore, brought much vitality to all the small communities.

J.O'H.: What, would you say, has kept your groups going over the years? Why have people kept coming to the meetings?

N.K.: One thing that David and I noted from the beginning was that our faith was nourished by the small Christian communities. When I went to the groups, I came back happier. I never felt that this was my project and that, if it didn't work, the failure was mine. You could feel the groups going by themselves almost. I sensed the Spirit was really working there and listening to the insights of people brought one truly in touch with the faith of the parishioners. The way we operated traditionally, the priest would be doing much work and a great deal of preaching, but there would be little feedback or little contact with the real faith of the people. I found the new rapport with the parishioners nourishing for myself. The members of the small communities in their evaluations also pointed out that they found it immensely helpful to hear other people talk about their problems and how the faith helped them in their lives. I would say, then, that the action of the Spirit was the main support in the groups. The social dimension was another: meeting people from the same street that you never knew were in the Church. In Freetown, Christians are very scattered. You might have one Catholic, for example, in a family that's entirely Muslim or one Catholic family on a street where all the other families are Muslim. Christians were isolated, and the opportunity to meet once a week with people of the same faith was, I think, a strong bond. What was it, therefore, that kept the groups going? In short I'd say the Spirit was urging us on and the small Christian community was a satisfying socio-religious experience. Furthermore, the small communities were part of a wider scene. That too was important to the people. They liked to refer to the fact that they were part of an international reality.

J.O'H.: How did you foster this wider vision?

N.K.: We did a lot to show what was happening in East Africa . . . ran off articles to give out in church . . . showed videos. National pastoral planning was focusing on the same point. There was a Lenten program with the theme *We are the Church*. We joined in with that . . . even sported T-shirts with the slogan and some interested folk wrote magazine articles on the topic. Parishioners vied with one another in pushing the program. You see, there are two sides to the parish, with the church in the middle. I don't know—they seem to enjoy competition.

J.O'H.: You hesitate, Noel. Would "emulation" be a better word?

N.K.: It would . . . good-natured emulation. One group would try some thing and they would be delighted with the results, so they'd want to share it with others. They would go across the parish, then, and say, "This is what we're doing" and they'd be happy about it. Or a member might go up country, to Koidu for example, and see something new. That person would then come back with the new idea. There was much cross-fertilization.

J.O'H.: Here and there you have touched on the subject of formation. Would you care to be specific?

N.K.: First of all David and myself had both been involved in formation work before coming to St. Martin's. We didn't have to bring resource people from outside. You were one of the few. David spent a great deal of time sharing on the Bible—his area of interest. DELTA of course was a factor in formation. We tried to set up a coordinating team for small Christian communities in the city of Freetown. In this way we would run training sessions for the whole city, rather than duplicate workshops. Every year we invited the participants in the courses at the Kenema Inter-territorial Pastoral Center to come to St. Martin's. They act as a catalyst. Help us to evaluate what is going on and come up with new ideas. They want to run workshops to share those ideas and we encourage them to do so. Generally we try to get a program of formation arranged at the beginning of the year. Anyway, formation is now largely in the hands of the coordinators of small Christian communities and the DELTA teams. They're deeply involved in the social aspect as well, so as to raise funds for the parish. They have this keen sense of responsibility; "We are Church," they say.

J.O'H.: It's wonderful that they are so imbued with the consciousness of being Church. . . . Any further item on formation?

N.K.: Well, David and I are leaving St. Martin's and a new team is moving in. . . . Oh, I hope, in fact I feel sure, that what's being done will continue. Much of the talent required to do this now exists in the parish. The resource persons within the parish may not be able to do everything themselves, but they can call on persons from the pastoral teams that function at national level. Furthermore, we have been striving to bring the parish council and the small Christian communities together for workshops. In this way the formation of the communities doesn't become a project separate from the parish council. On a number of occasions we have taken the whole parish council away on special workshops for two or three days. And we spent much time looking at what a parish council is and what small Christian communities and associations are. As a result the parish council has taken on a whole new lease on life.

J.O'H.: What sort of areas are covered in formation?

N.K.: Human relations in community, theology of community, small Christian communities, justice awareness, leadership skills, Scripture, Christian family life and so forth. The idea is to respond to what people feel they need and help them to enrich themselves.

J.O'H.: You have just been referring to the parish council and earlier you said that each small Christian community sends a representative to the council. Doesn't it become unwieldy? What if one day you have forty small communities?

N.K.: It hasn't been a problem. In the past we only had eight to ten groups. At the moment eight out of twelve groups are represented on the council. Elections are coming up soon though. In fact our parish council has 35 members.

J.O'H.: 35!

N.K.: It's not as overwhelming as it sounds. I'll explain; some of these are co-opted by the pastor . . . persons he thinks it would be good to have on, such as elders or wise people whose advice is highly valued. Others are elected by the various organizations. At any one meeting one finds about 20 representatives—a manageable number. Some of the 35 members don't take their responsibility that seriously. But we're happy. One can have a good workshop or meeting with 20; more than that creates problems. Everything has to be discussed and, if 35 people are discussing a topic, the dialogue can get out of control. As of now there is no danger of the parish council becoming unwieldy. The 12 small Christian communities we have are strategically located. They adequately cover the various areas of the parish. I can't see them subdividing much more, because Christians are quite scattered as it is and none of the groups is getting so big that it needs to subdivide. If there were ever to be 40 communities, one would certainly have to rationalize representation on the parish council.

J.O'H.: So 12 groups are quite adequate?

N.K.: Yes. With time it might conceivably go as far as 15 or 16, but 12 is a good number. We have some 3,000 parishioners; of these many don't go to church . . . once or twice a year maybe. If there is an average of 50 persons per small community—actually a core of 20 usually attend the weekly meetings while the remainder rally for tasks and key events—that's 600 people, which is quite a significant core.

J.O'H.: Noel, that bird outside the window has sung persistently all during your interview.

N.K.: Have you ever heard of the Zen Master who was about to deliver a sermon, when suddenly a bird sang? Whereupon the Master declared, "The sermon has been given," and sat down.

J.O'H.: In that case I must be grateful that you thought of this story at the end rather than at the beginning of our session.

7

Organizing Small Christian Communities

So far, apart from the stories of actual groups, we have considered some of the major features of the communities and looked at their theological background, the overall vision that is so important for the members. We now turn to organization.

Where organization is concerned, the guiding principle must be that it never becomes more important than persons: organization exists for persons, not persons for organization. Structures there must be, yet they must always be light. Now having said that, how does one go about starting a small Christian community?

STARTING

There is no blueprint for starting a small community. *We must start from where we are*. This means that local circumstances must be carefully borne in mind. Founding a group, for example, in an area where the Church has a long history is one thing; doing so where it is breaking new ground is quite another. Obviously, there is much more scope and freedom in the new situation.

And we cannot imagine that a model which works in one part of the world is totally suitable for another. The Brazilian model cannot be transferred totally to Ireland, or the United States model to Africa. That is not to say that a comparative study may not prove most enlightening.

It can be helpful if one develops a small Christian community around people who have already had a group experience of some sort. We saw this phenomenon at work in the stories of the St. Paul/Minneapolis, Crumlin and Colmena communities. Usually also there are common interests, such as a desire for fellowship, or social goals to be achieved. The social goals can be as basic as mending a road or as advanced as working for structures of society that are just. The following are examples of groups that have evolved into small Christian communities:

- Bible-study groups,
- RENEW groups,
- prayer, charismatic and catechetical groupings,
- neighborhood groups that come together to celebrate house Masses,
- discussion and problem-solving groups,
- groups that come together for a workshop, course or to do some practical task,
- close neighbors,
- migrants,
- persons of the same ethnic group—provided they remain entirely open to those of other ethnic origins.

In Africa it has also been:

- a core of the extended family,
- a group of the newly baptized,
- a nucleus of compound, village or outstation.

I recall one workshop that I was involved with in West Africa. Even while it was still in progress, three participants (Gloria, Honorius and Francis) were with infectious African enthusiasm already gathering neighbors in their compounds to relate to them what was happening at the workshop, and to join with them in reflection on the word of God and prayer.

If ordinary human cohesion is lacking, one cannot progress to Christian community. The walls of a house cannot be raised until the foundations are securely in place. I think of Dublin. Many people have been uprooted from communities with a long and rich tradition in the city center to be moved to faceless suburbs, where they are surrounded by strangers. This is a traumatic experience. The first task in a situation like that has to be a fostering of basic human relationships. So one would strive to bring people together on whatever basis: recreational, social, political. . . . Bingo could well be the starting point or it could be a matter of groups organizing to obtain amenities.

A final point. Rather than start with one small Christian community, it is better, if at all possible, to begin with a couple at least. The small Christian community needs a mirror image to help it towards maturity. The reader will recall how the Freetown groups challenged and helped one another.

COMPOSITION

Since the small Christian community is a cell of the Church, it should be open to every Christian irrespective of race, color, sex, calling or whatever. Normally, of course, the groups are associated with an area so the members tend to be from the same background.

In certain places, too, there may be factors at work which render it necessary, as part of a process, to live for a time with something that falls short of the ideal. There are parts of Africa, rural areas in particular, where it is hard for the youth to participate in the small Christian communities. Traditionally youth remain silent in the presence of their elders. What could be done in this situation is that the young people form their own small communities and meet on occasions with the adults in order to share with them. In this way the groups remain open to one another, and with time, barriers will, we hope, be overcome.

Irrespective of whether they are part of the small Christian communities or not, youth do need their own Christian groups to deal with the issues proper to that stage of life. And the same may be true for women. Although part of the small Christian communities, they may need their own Christian groupings to deal with the challenges peculiar to their situation.

Regarding children, one notices a healthy tendency in the small Christian communities to be mindful of their needs and, where possible, to involve them in meetings and activities. Some French communities, for example, came together for a weekend and much of the time was devoted to entertaining and being with the children. At the beginning of a meeting in Ghana, I recall that the children were invited to sing and share before the adults launched into their discussion. Indeed, little children are very much in evidence at small community meetings in Africa.

LEADERSHIP

Competent leadership is essential to the smooth running of a small Christian community. In our day such leadership is largely a question of animation and coordination, certainly not of domination.

I was once at a small Christian community meeting where a rather overpowering leader harangued the participants for at least 45 minutes on the matter under consideration.

After that he asked if anyone had anything to say. Nobody had anything to say. In fact there was nothing left to say.

The effective leader is not like that. She is not out in front pulling people after her, nor behind pushing people in front. The good leader is one who walks shoulder to shoulder with others, encouraging them to go forward of their own accord. She is not an intrusive presence.

What the leader of a community must do is help it to run its affairs on the basis of dialogue and consensus—a process which requires great maturity in the members. They have to sit down in a prayerful atmosphere and calmly talk matters out together so that they come to an agreement as to what to do. The leaders normally make decisions in line with the consensus.

This consensus model of ordering affairs is achieved through conscientious, honest, open dialogue. Force, manipulation and unsavory horse-trading are studiously avoided. It is characterized by a genuine desire to discern the will of God through the guidance of the Holy Spirit. Paul VI says that it is through "trustful dialogue" in community that the will of God is discovered for a community (cf. *Evangelica Testificatio*, 25).[42] So we see the vital importance of the community meeting and of the dialogue which takes place there.

Dialogue is not simply a matter of speaking; even more so is it a matter of careful listening. It demands that we stand in the shoes of the other person. Such an ability to listen will help to prevent the members from stubbornly persisting in entrenched positions and will foster a mature spirit of give-and-take.

Nor is consensus majority rule. All the members of a group must work to come to an agreement. There may be a couple of persons who have deep reservations about a course which a community is proposing. These owe it to the Holy Spirit, the community and themselves to voice their opinions. Indeed, assemblies have been turned right round by timely or prophetic interventions. Yet if the community, having duly considered their viewpoint, still feels that the proposed course ought to be followed, then the persons concerned must be sensitive to the way in which the Spirit is moving the consensus.

As an example of a prophetic intervention, I would like to recall an incident that happened in West Africa. The coordinator for a community was being elected, and a man was on the verge of being chosen. One of the participants then remarked that the group had been speaking a lot about truly valuing its womenfolk and proposed that they elect a woman – a novelty for the locality in question, to say the least. So voting began anew, and a woman was speedily elected.

What if the members of the small community cannot reach a consensus? Where the approach is mature and conscientious, such an impasse is highly unlikely. If it should happen, however, they might fruitfully focus on what it is that is dividing them to see if they cannot remove the obstacle. If they are still unable to remove it, they might come to a decision on the basis of the areas on which they already agree. And then they can await developments, or come to an interim decision, regarding the area that is proving to be difficult.

The reader will have realized by now that one of the most important qualities of the good leader is an ability to animate dialogue. She should encourage people to speak freely, yet not shoot off at irrelevant tangents. A leader must keep the discussion on course and urge the members towards decision and action.

AUTHORITARIANISM

Dialogue, or anything else for that matter, is not helped by a dominating leader. "We are all in this together," a leader of a community once said, speaking of an emergency, "right from myself *down* to the last person in this room." This was hardly a statement to encourage fruitful dialogue. If there is one thing that can be said about leadership nowadays, it is that authoritarianism doesn't succeed. Young people, particularly, reject it. In doing so, whether or not they know it, they show a sure evangelical instinct. Their quarrel is not with authority understood as service, but with authority understood as dominance. In this they are in line with the Gospel:

> You know that the rulers of the gentiles lord it over them, and their great men exercise authority over them. It shall not be so among you; but whoever would be great among you must be your servant, and whoever would be first among you must be your slave; even as the Son of man came not to be served but to serve, and to give his life as a ransom for many. (Matthew 20:25–28)

Most Christians would agree with the statement that authority is for service. It is our understanding and, consequently, practice of service which goes awry. In effect, we can practice dominance and call it service.

A TEAM OF LEADERS

It is better to have a little team of leaders rather than a solitary one in a small Christian community. There may be practical reasons for this. Many small Christian communities flourish around mines and factories where there is shift work, and one or another leader is in the factory or down in the mine while the meeting of the group is in progress. If there is only one leader, this can be inconvenient.

Usually the leadership in a community is renewed with regularity. If there is a team, not all leaders are changed together. This facilitates renewal yet at the same time assures continuity.

There is an even more compelling reason. Where there is only one leader (animator, coordinator), she may adopt a proprietary attitude towards the group and even begin to speak of "my community."

I recall being in a praesidium of the Legion of Mary as a boy, and I remember how our president used to refer to us as "my legionnaires." I immediately used to have visions of myself on some distant desert rampart, repelling oncoming hordes, as faithful comrades dropped all about me. A community or a praesidium, of course, is not the possession of one person; it belongs to all the members.

A team can help in avoiding this problem, and it achieves something still more important. It preserves the principle and witness of community even in the leadership. In other words, the community is animated by a community.

DUTIES OF THE LEADERS

Leaders perform a variety of tasks such as the following:

- summoning, planning and directing meetings,
- conducting celebrations of the word of God,
- leading prayer,
- distributing communion,
- organizing retreats, days of reflection, workshops, courses,
- organizing the activities (apostolate) of the group,
- making time to chat personally with members regarding joys, sorrows, achievements, problems/opportunities,
- facilitating social events,
- and encouraging ministries.

MINISTRIES

One can confidently expect God to bless a small Christian community with the ministries that it needs to function. The members possess gifts or charisms that become ministries when the community publicly commissions them to use those gifts or charisms in the service of the Kingdom. Thus we find people talented at

- music,
- interpreting the Bible,
- spontaneous prayer,
- conducting religious education,
- working with young people,

- working for justice,
- practicing hospitality, sociability,
- helping the old, the sick, the imprisoned.

Need I add here that we are not speaking of ministry in the strict sense, that is, of ministry such as diaconate or priesthood which comes with ordination. There is no question of ordination where the ministries we refer to are concerned—a commissioning, yes. Such a commissioning is becoming more common in the Church today. Lectors and eucharistic ministers are usually mandated at formal ceremonies to exercise these roles.

ROLE OF THE BISHOP

Thus far we have been speaking of the leadership in the small Christian community, though what has been said is valid for all Christian leadership.

The bishop, of course, is the key figure of the diocesan community and of the parish communities and small Christian communities which go to form it. The bishop is the sign of unity who does the following:

- coordinates and animates in God's name,
- serves,
- teaches,
- guides,
- governs (always in a context of service),
- approves of,
- and relates not only small Christian communities but communities of all kinds (small, area, parish, diocese) to one another and to the Church at large.

The role finds its inspiration in the Vatican II document on the Church, *Lumen Gentium*:

> the bishops received the charge of the community, presiding in God's stead over the flock of which they are shepherds in that they are teachers of doctrine, ministers of sacred worship and holders of office in government.[43]

The Pope, as successor of Peter and Bishop of Rome, is concerned for the unity of the whole Church (cf. Matthew 16:18–

20), and a test as to whether any diocese in the world is on the right path is that it be in communion with Rome on truths that really matter. The bishops too, as successors of the apostles in their own right, must share this worldwide task and concern with the Pope (cf. Matthew 18:18).

It is obvious that the bishop alone cannot handle all that has to be done in a diocese. Helpers such as priests and deacons are required. There was a far greater proportion of bishops to faithful in the early Church than there is today. Consequently, they knew their people intimately. Owing to administrative burdens, the bishop in time became sadly distanced from his people. This is a grave disadvantage.

Briefly, then, the services rendered by the priest and deacon, as helpers, to the small Christian communities are similar to those of the bishop.

A final word on the subject of authority. We have seen that the Gospel undoubtedly understands authority in terms of service. But service can be understood in various ways. We normally think of service as doing things for others. Yet, perhaps even more so, service can be a matter of challenging others and enabling them to do things for themselves. Jesus did things for others: he washed the disciples' feet (cf. John 13:1–20). Yet he challenged: "Are you able to drink the cup that I am to drink?" he asked James and John (Matthew 20:22). And they did. Even in the act of doing something for people, he urged them to move on their own behalf: "Rise, take up your bed, and go home," he told the paralytic (Matthew 9:6).

NETWORKING

As with leadership, networking is an important organizational factor in small Christian communities. They must forge links between themselves so as to get a sense of being a communion of communities. There follow some suggestions, upon which the reader can enlarge, as to how this might be done. It is a random selection after the manner of a brainstorming.

- Create situations for coming together, for example, liturgical or social celebrations.

- Foster communication among groups through a newsletter or magazine.
- Share books, publications, photocopied material, and so on.
- Share audio-visuals: films, slide shows, videos, and so forth.
- Draw up a directory of small Christian communities.
- Enter the details of existing groups onto a computer.
- Engage in correspondence or use the telephone or radio.
- Make use of the resource persons who circulate to share with small Christian communities at local, diocesan, national or international levels.
- Seek knowledge together: through Bible courses, courses in theology (the faith basis for living) and so on.
- Avail of pastors, parish councils and diocesan bodies as focal points.
- Have an understanding regarding prayer; for example, the members of a number of communities could decide, no matter where they found themselves, to pause briefly and pray for each other at noon each day. Or they could have prayers in common, even though they might not be physically present to one another.
- Have a conscious awareness that all over the globe there are small communities that are striving for a better world.
- Avail of the organized Church itself as a context for the communities; the parish, for example, can become a communion of communities. This has the merit of *starting from where we are* for the most part.
- Utilize small Christian communities as instruments for evangelization, catechesis, conscientization, inculturation, communication and promoting justice. As such they will inevitably forge links.
- Arrange encounters at parish, diocesan, national and international levels—simple encounters, not lavish or expensive affairs.
- Share apostolic activities; for example, youth work or development projects.
- Let members circulate between small communities to share ideas. This leads to a healthy emulation.

Then there can be an environment of harmony in society generally that, if created, could be favorable to networking among small Christian communities. There are various contributions that small communities themselves can make towards promoting this atmosphere:

- Cultivate attitudes that will remove the barriers that society has erected on grounds of race, so-called class, sex, religion or whatever.
- Promote family life and relate families to one another as a foundation for community building.
- Support activities that can bring about camaraderie: sport, recreation, clubs, drama, music and so forth.
- Foster attitudes of openness, tolerance, participation and inclusiveness.
- Believe in the dialogue and consensus approach to decision making.
- Abhor authoritarianism, paternalism, domination and manipulation that are so opposed to the spirit of the Gospel.

A meeting of Italian small Christian communities in 1973 described how they hoped to meet their goals:

> We are working to build a Church that . . . is the horizontal communion of believing communities . . . spread throughout the world and hidden in the world as a ferment. They will be united by functional interlinking, not power, in the service of common liberation.[44]

This provides an interesting perspective. As I see it, the description envisions clusters of small Christian communities at the grassroots linked together across the world, yet linked only in a manner that is necessary for the promotion of the Kingdom of God and not for the purpose of building a power structure.

ZONING

Sometimes a parish is zoned into a number of divisions that are then considered small Christian communities. The problem in doing this is that there is the danger of drawing demarcation lines through natural human and Christian groupings. The diagram on page 107 represents a parish that has been wrongly divided in this fashion.

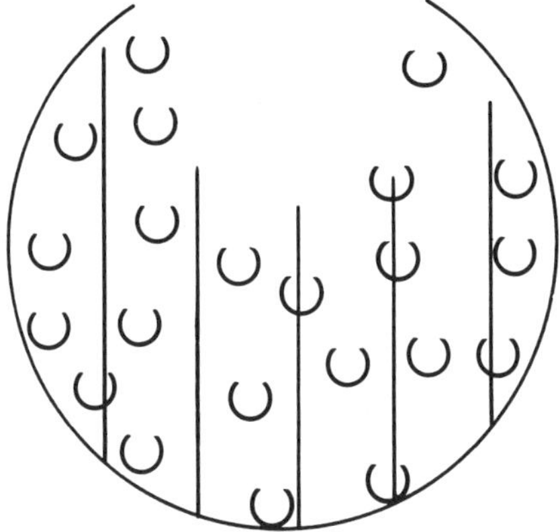

There is also the misconception here that small Christian community has to do with territory and not with people. It might be wise, therefore, because of the danger of splitting spontaneous groupings, simply to float the idea of forming small Christian communities. Then folk can be allowed to find the rallying points with which they feel most comfortable. Presumably these will be in their own areas. There is hardly a point in persons uprooting themselves from where circumstances have planted them and God wants them to grow.

FORMATION

After they had survived their various ups and downs for a number of years, I once asked the Colmena small Christian community what it was that kept them going. The response was unanimous. It was the formation that they had received and were receiving.

The word "formation" can have overtones of manipulation by others. But so too can "training," "education" or "instruction." It is what actually happens that matters. The formation that we are talking about here is ultimately auto-formation, or formation that comes largely from within oneself. In other words the subject desires and participates actively and critically in the educational process: it is a question of self-enrichment.

Since formation in this sense can be so helpful, we must necessarily dwell on the topic. There has, of course, to be initial and ongoing formation and it has to be formation in the fullest sense: spiritual, creative, intellectual, human. . . .

Much formation comes through dialogue at meetings and, for that matter, through casual conversation. With time, however, the members of a community usually request a more organized approach as well. As a result of encounters and discussions in their places of work or study, they may, for example, realize their deficiencies regarding the Bible or religious knowledge and ask for a solid grounding in the one or the other. The Freetown experience is a case in point. This provides the opportunity for a competent person (lay, clerical or religious) to step in and meet a vital need. Among the means for meeting such needs are courses, seminars, retreats, days of recollection, lectures, audio-visual materials, and various types of literature.

Formation can be provided in such areas as small Christian community, Bible, basic theology, justice and peace, social teaching of the Church, catechetics, integral development, leadership skills, group dynamics, counseling and so forth.

There are often pastoral centers where people can go for such courses. There are also resource persons or teams who move about giving courses to the communities. There is need for both approaches. One advantage of taking courses to the groups is that entire small Christian communities can benefit from them, which is useful since leadership circulates in communities. Normally key individuals are selected to go to pastoral centers. These persons, however, should do courses with a view to going back and sharing all that they have learned with their groups. And it would be better if a team of two were to go rather than just one person. They support each other when they return home.

One of the most enriching factors in a small Christian community is the reflection–action process, already referred to, that penetrates ever more deeply into the problem situation. The community doesn't simply do things; it continually reflects on what it does, and continually goes out to do better. In this reflection–action approach consists the so-called process of *conscien-*

tization. Conscientization raises our awareness, but with a view to changing the world.

An example may help to explain what conscientization means. A small Christian community decided to give the poorest of the poor children of the area a little present for a festive occasion.

Reflecting on this action at their weekly meeting, the members were happy with the way it went. After much discussion, however, one person remarked on the reaction of the children's parents. They had stood by looking rather gloomy. The ingratitude of it!

None too quickly it dawned on them that maybe the parents were mortified because they themselves were not giving their own children the presents.

So next time round the small Christian community secretly supplied the gifts to the mothers and fathers, who then went on to present them to their own children.

In the following meeting the group agreed that this proved much more successful. But then someone wondered why it was that those parents could not afford even a small gift for their own children. By dint of reflection and action the community was getting to the heart of the social problem.

I should like to give a further example of the action–reflection dynamic, or conscientization process, at work. It is about Patricia, who lived in a poor South American *barrio*. Her brother-in-law was in prison. He was there because he physically assaulted her husband. Remarkable Christian that she was, Patricia forgave him and wanted him released. A police official told her that he could have this arranged, but demanded a considerable sum of money. Patricia scrimped and scraped until she had the required amount and then presented it to the official in question. He pocketed the money and did absolutely nothing about the release of Patricia's brother-in-law.

When she told me about this, I was truly indignant. "Patricia, you have been treated terribly unjustly," I declared.

"Yes, yes, *padrecito*," she replied, "I know that." Yet as I observed her closely, I got a sense that she didn't understand. The word "justice" held no real meaning for her. What I had done was suddenly flash an intense light in the eyes of one who had spent all her life in the darkness of oppression, just as her forebears had done for hundreds of years. She simply could not take in the meaning of what I was saying.

Patricia, however, became part of a small community and eight years later I heard her quietly announce: "I have learned many things by being part of this community." Indeed she had. This was the result of meetings, courses, social action and much dialogue and reflection regarding the action taken. Through all of these her consciousness was raised and she became a fully conscientized, or aware, woman. And a valiant one at that. But all this had happened ever so gradually.

The pastoral planning method, given in chapter 9, provides a practical application of the conscientizing, or action–reflection, process. Above all one acquires a sense of its gradualness.

I often feel that the process of conscientization (reflection–action) is the world's best university, for it certainly takes one far. Some of the most educated people, regarding the world and how it functions in religious, political, social and economic terms, whom I have met have been poor *campesinos* (peasants) in Ecuador and factory workers on the outskirts of São Paulo. In a real sense they were far more educated, thanks to conscientization, than even professional people whom I have encountered elsewhere. These latter could be most proficient in their calling, yet quite limited in their knowledge of the workings of society.

A SENSE OF PROCESS

We see, therefore, that from the outset a small Christian community should have a sense of gradualness, or process; a realization that growth doesn't happen overnight but is the work of years. True progress is neither unduly rushed nor unduly delayed. It proceeds at a proper pace.

Practically this means that the small Christian community

- takes people where they are,
- challenges them to grow as persons,
- and strives to create the environment of love and acceptance that alone makes growth possible.

When we proceed in this way, we are only imitating the manner in which God deals with all of us. God accepts and loves us as we are, challenges us through the Gospel to grow and gives us a loving Christian family and community to help us in our endeavors. So God is most respectful of the person, and the Christian community must be the same.

The maturing that takes place in a small Christian community can be rather like what takes place in the life of the human person. Childhood can be pleasant and protected—unfortunately it is not so for the vast majority of the world's children—adolescence vulnerable and problematic, adulthood stable. Which does not mean, of course, that adulthood is problem free, only that grown-ups can, hopefully, cope more successfully with their difficulties.

Having a sense of process then can prevent much frustration in a small Christian community. We will not expect people to run before they have learned to walk. We are not of course making a case for foot-dragging. Our age is one of headlong change, typified by a celebrity who reputedly stuck a pie into a microwave oven, then stamped her feet and yelled, "What's the delay!" They say that changes which formerly took a hundred years now happen in ten. Viewed from this perspective, it is 250 years since Vatican II. So to cope with our world we must have an abiding sense of urgency and be eternally adaptable.

Change is of course never easy and there are those who find it exceedingly difficult. Nevertheless, while we affirm those values that are sound for every era, we had better make the inevitable adjustments that are part of human destiny. Cardinal Newman wisely remarked: "In a higher world it is otherwise; but here below to live is to change, and to be perfect is to have changed often."[45]

SUMMARY

1. We must start small Christian community from where we are, taking local circumstances very much into account.
2. It is helpful to start with people who have some experience of living and working together. Existing groups can prove a good starting point.
3. There is normally a common interest or social concern among those who wish to begin.

4. In situations where people are alienated (e.g., impersonal suburbs) the first step towards eventually forming small Christian communities could be the bringing together of people on any basis whatsoever (e.g., recreational) to foster basic human relationships.
5. Competent leadership (that animates and coordinates, not dominates) is essential for the smooth running of a small Christian community.
6. The leader must help the community to run its affairs on the basis of dialogue and consensus. The dialogue–consensus approach calls for conscientious, honest, open discussion. It requires maturity.
7. It is through "trustful dialogue" in a community that the will of God is discovered for a community (cf. *Evangelica Testificatio*, 25). Hence the importance of the community meeting.
8. Authoritarianism (domination) doesn't succeed—authority is for service (cf. Matthew 20:25–28).
9. It is better to have a team of leaders rather than a solitary leader. This means that:
   - responsibilities are shared,
   - the possible attitude of possessiveness that an individual leader can develop towards a group is avoided,
   - and the witness of community is present even in the leadership.
10. The duties of leaders are varied (examples given).
11. Ministries are gifts or charisms that the members of a community can have (examples provided). The leaders must help the members to discover their gifts and the community must publicly commission their use.
12. The bishop, priest and deacon are key figures for the small Christian communities. They
    - coordinate and animate in God's name,
    - serve,
    - teach,
    - govern (always in a context of service),
    - approve of and relate small Christian communities of all kinds to one another and to the Church at large.
13. The Pope is concerned with the unity of the whole Church

(cf. Matthew 16:18–20). The bishops share this responsibility with him (cf. Matthew 18:18). The dioceses of the world must be in communion with Rome.

14. Networking is important for the small Christian communities (some possible means to achieve this are cited).
15. There must be initial and ongoing formation (understood as auto-formation, or self-enrichment) in the small community. Formation is in the fullest sense: spiritual, creative, intellectual and human.
16. One of the most enriching factors in the group is the reflection-action procedure that it adopts—the process of conscientization.
17. A small Christian community must develop a sense of process—the realization that growth is gradual and can neither be unduly rushed nor unduly delayed.
18. While affirming eternal values, the members had better be able to make the changes that the times demand.

8

The Small Christian Community Meeting

The staple components of the small Christian community meeting are as follows:
• reality,
• the word of God,
• community.
All these components are vital. The word of God is central, but it has to be related to the lives and concerns of the participants. And the gathering cannot be just an amalgam of individuals; rather it must be a meeting of people who are striving to share deeply all aspects of their lives.

The reader may be wondering about the place of the Eucharist in the meeting of the small Christian community. The Eucharist is of course the most consummate expression of community; it is also a celebration of harmony. Yet, desirable though it may be, it is not easy at present to organize the celebration of the Eucharist for small Christian community meetings. It is possible on occasions, and certainly the members should attend and animate the Sunday assemblies.

The meeting ought to respond to real needs. One night the community may be planning its work (apostolate), and the meeting is devoted to that particular task. Next time the session could be devoted to analyzing a problem. There is, in other words, freedom and flexibility in organizing the sessions.

Needs decide the agenda of a meeting: there ought to be no rigid pattern. This does not mean that sessions are unplanned. Quite the contrary. In fact, the preparation has to be more thorough than when there is a regular format. Generally at the end of a meeting the participants decide the subject for the next.

A group of course may want to have an ongoing theme for those moments when nothing of urgency presents itself. A community I know has decided to work systematically through the Vatican II document on the laity, *Apostolicam Actuositatem*.

In practice I find that groups can easily slip into a routine of Bible reflection and prayer in their meetings and lose flexibility. Since the small Christian community is a cell of the Church and has many varied aspects, to get into any routine may limit possibilities. I realize of course that flexibility is not easy, especially at the outset, when people are looking for something to hold on to; yet it should be worked towards. Communities are greatly helped by the participation of a resource person in their meetings, particularly in the early days.

When we think of meetings, we usually think of formal gatherings. Yet our lives are made up of rather more casual encounters: relaxed meetings at work, running into friends on the street, a game of cards or chess, study groups, meetings to prepare for or celebrate the sacraments, cultural or religious functions, outings, holidays and pilgrimages. All these can help considerably in forging community. We should be aware of this. Indeed, when members reflect on factors that keep them together over long periods, apart from spiritual considerations, purely social encounters are very much to the fore. But, then, Christ himself loved to sit and eat and chat with people. And he provided the drinks for what must have been one of the earliest recorded cocktail parties!

THE WORD OF GOD

Regarding the word of God, it is important to realize that it doesn't take precedence over the life experience of the members of a community. They must look first at their own lives and try to make sense of them in the light of the Scriptures, just as the early Christians looked first of all at their own life experiences and then sought to interpret and make sense of them in the light of the whole Christ-event. The Spirit of Christ is not only found in Scripture but also in the Christian community of every era. As Carlos Mesters, a Dutch scholar and missionary working in Brazil, puts it: "the word of God is not just the Bible. The word of God is within reality and it can be discovered there with the help of the Bible."[46] Simply put, the word of God only comes to life when practiced. So, ideally, to use the Scriptures effectively, a community should meet around the word of God, yet relate the realities of their own lives to the text: "Their struggle becomes part of the picture."[47] Put yet another way, the word of God is not the word of God when it remains in a book or on the lips. It only becomes truly the word of God when the blood of humanity rushes through its veins.

An interesting phenomenon of our times is that the Bible is to be found back in the hands of the laity. It is no longer the preserve of just the cleric and the scholar. This is a wholesome development because the Bible was written by ordinary people and for ordinary people in the first place. And common folk can be more at home than the sophisticated with the stories, myths, symbols, songs, poems, dramas and powerful word pictures that are the very stuff of which the Scriptures are made. The academic, for example, might tie himself up in knots wondering as to how Jesus walked on the water whereas the ordinary person will take this in his or her stride and go straight to the underlying message. In listening for many years to poor people reflecting on the Bible, I, like many others, have been impressed by the wisdom of their interventions.

If, therefore, there is a person with a knowledge of the background of the Bible in a small Christian community, how can he best help the group? One thing is certain: he must beware of taking over the meeting and turning it into a Bible lesson, thereby stifling the spontaneity and participation of the members. He could help, however, by briefly providing something of the historical or cultural background of the passage under consideration.

We see Ernesto Cardenal do this very skillfully with the peasants of Solentiname in Nicaragua. The community is about to discuss Matthew 6:7–15, or the Our Father if one prefers. Taking the words:

> And in prayer
> do not heap up empty phrases,

Ernesto goes on to explain, "The translation is rather, 'Don't go blah-blah-blah-blah.' The Greek word that Matthew uses is *battalogein*, which is like saying 'blah-blah-blah-blah.'" Then dealing with the opening expression:

> Our Father who art in heaven,

he further elaborates: "Jesus didn't really use the word 'Father.' Jesus said in Aramaic *Abba*, which is 'papa,' and that was probably always the word he used in speaking of God."[48]

With this introduction, the stage is set for a most absorbing reflection by the participants.

Finally, the most effective way to use the Scriptures in the small communities is for the members to ask how the passage in hand questions or challenges them. A methodology for breaking open the word of God is suggested in Appendix 1.

SAMPLE MEETINGS

I shall now give a sampling in note form of ten meetings. Some are of the same type, but for the most part they are different. The intention is that they may serve as examples, or paradigms, to spark off possibilities in the mind of the group leader/animator, not that they be adhered to exactly. The sessions that follow are based on meetings that have actually taken place.

MEETING ONE: AN EXERCISE

The basis of this meeting takes the form of an *exercise*, or group dynamic, to help the members of a community relate to one another. It is particularly good when a group is in its early stages.

1. The Exercise

a. The leader/animator of the meeting asks all present to think about the question, Who am I? (10–15 min. approx.).

b. Each member is asked to seek out a person whom he or she would like to know better. They chat with each other about themselves. They will, it is hoped, reveal some of their feelings (when feelings are revealed we get to know each other better). Interesting details can add spice. They also discuss what they would like to gain from being in community (10–15 min. approx.).

c. The leader calls upon the groups of two to join other pairs so as to make groups of four. The participants chat, not about themselves this time but about their partners of the previous step. Points of interest regarding persons are noted. And they are asked to decide as a group what they would like to gain from being in community (20 min. approx.).

d. The groups of four now join to form groups of eight and the introductions are repeated in these enlarged groups. Then each group chooses a person to animate the proceedings and another to make notes. They share the group expectations for community as decided in the previous steps (20 min. approx.).

e. All join in a general session. But the groups of eight remain together. The person who has been noting the proceedings says a little about the participants in his or her group. Then the leader calls upon the groups to share four or five major expectations that they have for the community. These are written up on a blackboard and discussed.

2. Apt Scripture reading (cf. Appendix 1).

Having seen how the Scripture might shed light on the discussion, the community ought to think of some action it could take as a result of the session. This might be something entirely new or it could be a matter of intensifying action already being taken.

3. Shared prayer and hymn.

Note: The above exercise follows the pattern of human relationships. First we are alone. Then we open to another (mother), to a limited group (family) and finally to the whole community. Exercises or group dynamics can be a fruitful source for meetings.

MEETING TWO: AN EXERCISE

These are notes on a recent meeting conducted by a Dublin small Christian community. I found the session most interesting and well prepared. Again, it was based on an *exercise*, or group dynamic, the purpose being on this occasion to highlight the importance of self-confidence.

1. Check in: each member was asked to say something about how he or she felt at the moment (earth-shaking revelations were not expected).
2. There were musical chairs to enliven the proceedings. I hasten to add that all the participants were youthful, so there were no sprained ankles.
3. Soap-box activity: each member was in turn seated on a central chair and asked to speak on a topic that he or she picked out of a hat. There were such items as:
   - sliced bread,
   - socks,
   - ashtray,
   - banana,
   - curtains,
   - giraffe (this subject fell to my lot and stretched me considerably).

Though youthful, the group is quite experienced and it was amazing to discover how inventive and articulate they were in speaking about these topics.

The leader/animator of the meeting pointed out that the topics were trivial and caused a lot of mirth. However, if people could speak on these, they could surely speak on anything. Another member pointed out that it was good to have been put on the spot, because spontaneity helps self-confidence.

4. There followed a more thorough debriefing in which the following items were noted:
   - the need for people to affirm one another,
   - the importance of attentiveness,

- how necessary it is to have a certain inner toughness and not be overly sensitive,
- the need to believe in oneself,
- and how important community and family are for all of us.

5. A selection of mottoes was then read out. Each member was asked to reflect on them and choose one that appealed to her or him. Here are some examples of the mottoes:

   Let us be grateful for every single minute of this wonderful day!

   An optimist is someone who takes the cold water thrown upon an idea, heats it with enthusiasm and then uses the steam to push ahead.

   Help me to remember, God, that there isn't anything that can happen today that you and me [sic] can't handle.

6. Bible reflection: Matthew 6:25–34. This is the beautiful passage that tells us how God looks after the birds of the air and the flowers of the field. Much more so, then, will that God look after all of us; and there in a nutshell is the ultimate reason why we face the ups and downs of life with self-confidence. Motivated with this thought, the members of the community determined to strive to bring a spirit of self-confidence into all that they did.
7. The leader then played a recording of Julie Andrews' spunky version of "I Have Confidence" from *The Sound of Music*.
8. Check out: this was a mixture of spontaneous prayer and prayerful reflections. At the very end all linked hands and recited the Our Father.

MEETING THREE: COMMITMENT

To reflect upon and deepen the understanding of commitment is of the utmost importance for a small Christian community. Commitment is the soul of community. This meeting has to do with *commitment*.

Procedure:

Following the method given in Appendix 1, the participants share a Bible reflection on Mark 10:17–31, which is about the Rich Young Man who was called to commitment. This provides the opportunity for the participants to examine what is involved in the area of commitment and can result in an excellent meeting.

MEETING FOUR: PROPHETIC

What follows is the outline for a *prophetic* meeting, or a meeting to do with a justice issue. It is dealing with the problem of a poorly maintained road in the township of an African city, so bad that a toddler has nearly drowned in a pothole. The outline:

1. Opening prayer.
2. Discussion of problem: what action is to be taken? Will the members of the community take the matter in hand and do something themselves? Or will they protest to the municipal council? Send a delegation with thousands of signatures? They must decide.
3. Following the deliberations, a Bible reading may throw light on their situation, for example, Luke 3:1–6. This passage speaks about "the rough ways being made smooth." If the way for Jesus is to be properly prepared, the paths must be straight—there must be justice.
4. Shared prayer.

MEETING FIVE: PLANNING

Let us suppose that the small Christian community referred to in the previous prophetic meeting has decided to protest to an unsympathetic municipal council about the neglect of their road. Let us further suppose that the members have already collected a lengthy list of signatures. They now meet to plan their encounter with the chairman of the municipal council. This is an example of how this *planning* session might go.

1. Opening prayer.
2. In the course of discussion the members do the following:
   - decide whether the entire small Christian community or sim-

ply a representation will go to the encounter with the chairman of the municipal council,

- work out what they wish to say,
- appoint a spokesperson who will present the case and submit the list of signatures,
- decide if and where to meet beforehand for a short Bible reading and prayer,
- arrange a place to meet if they are not to come together for the Bible sharing and prayer session,
- decide when they will evaluate the meeting with the chairperson of the municipal council (at their next session?),

3. Bible sharing—1 Peter 3:13–18 ("make a defense to anyone who calls you to account for the hope that is in you . . ."). A most apt passage.
4. Shared prayer.

MEETING SIX: EVALUATION

Small Christian communities must evaluate every aspect of their lives. For this they have *evaluation* sessions. It is yet another type of meeting.

1. Opening prayer, hymn.
2. For the evaluation the group will use the questionnaires set out in Appendix 2. Obviously there is too much here for one meeting. I should think that the work could be spread over about three sessions.
3. Bible reflection—Acts 15 (the disciples evaluate).
4. Shared prayer, hymn.

Note: At least once a year a small Christian community should completely evaluate itself. Partial evaluations are more frequent. Indeed, through its reflection–action approach the small community is in a sense continually evaluating itself.

MEETING SEVEN: ECUMENICAL

A small Christian community, composed of Catholics, is to meet with some Protestant neighbors who are seeking information on small community with a view to setting up their own. This is an *ecumenical* session that might possibly take this course:

1. Opening prayer and hymn: "Father, we adore you."
2. Introductions. Each person introduces himself or herself.
3. The members of the existing small Christian community composed of Catholics might
   - share their experience with their Protestant neighbors;
   - offer them help in forming their own small Christian communities;
   - explore the possibilities of sharing worship on occasions;
   - and explore the possibility of doing work together for the good of the neighborhood.
4. Bible sharing—John 17:19–23 ("that they may be one").
5. Shared prayer, hymn ("Bind us together"), sign of peace.

MEETING EIGHT: WORSHIP

A small Christian community is languishing and feels the need for a spiritual fillip, so they decide to devote a whole meeting to the celebration of the Eucharist. It is a *worship* session. The participation of all the members is desirable and they must bear in mind items such as these:

- getting ready the place of celebration,
- preparing the music and hymns,
- enumerating the good things (e.g., friendship) which they wish to celebrate,
- taking care of readings and bidding prayers,
- having an offertory procession,
- introducing a mime—at the offertory usually,
- giving a communion reflection.

MEETING NINE: WORSHIP

A further *worship* meeting. These are notes that I made on yet another meeting of the Dublin group mentioned above.

1. Check-in: the members related what had happened in their lives since their last meeting. Their lives were busy and full of ups and downs.
2. The leader/animator announced that the bulk of the meeting would be devoted to personal reflection and prayer. A selection of stimulating reading material was placed on a table. A

letter supposedly from Jesus Christ was set up in one corner of the room with a few colorful votive candles near it. In the letter Christ reminded the reader of the personal friendship between them and wondered if in the hurly-burly of life he or she had found time to talk with him. The members were free just to sit and meditate, could browse through the materials provided, go read the letter or visit a nearby chapel.

3. After about an hour the members were asked if they might not like to share something with the community. One member said that in the course of the meditation she thought of the people she loved and of those who loved her. Often in daily dealings with them she became overly aware of their faults; the meditation restored a proper perspective, so that she saw the goodness more clearly. A second member said that she felt relaxed and happy. A third person informed us that he had spent the whole previous evening discussing God with his friends. On reflection, however, he realized that the only one whose words were not considered in the discussion was, in fact, God. Again, he said that the meeting put things in perspective. And so it went.
4. The Bible reading was from Ecclesiastes 3:1–9 ("For everything there is a season"). The members reflected that in the welter of activities that went to make their daily lives they must be careful not to forget their Friend (God/Jesus). There must be the restoring moments in order to go to the mountaintop or desert place and get a perspective on what really matters in life. The session gradually wound to an end in a mixture of reflection and prayer.

MEETING TEN: MISCELLANEOUS

I should like to remark, finally, that I have seen good meetings develop from *miscellaneous* sources: songs, poems, stories, slide projections, films, and so on. Analyzing a story for its meaning is a good exercise insofar as it helps us to do the same with the Bible, which also has a strong element of story. The format for any of these sources could be:

1. Opening prayer or hymn.

2. The story is read or related, song played, poem recited, film projected.
3. There is discussion of the questions and issues that the story or song or whatever raises for the lives of the members.
4. A suitable passage from Scripture is now read and the members reflect upon it. They then come up with something practical that can be done as a result of the discussion and Bible-sharing.
5. Shared prayer. (4 and 5 are often intermingled.)

One hopes that the foregoing examples may be of assistance to people in small Christian communities. In the last analysis, however, there are no great complications involved in the sessions. All over the world today thousands of simple communities will gather, talk about their lives in the light of the Gospel, pray and determine what action they will take to build up the Kingdom of God. And some of them may never even have heard the term *group dynamic*.

A final observation: as a small Christian community begins it will be good to give due attention to such key themes as community, commitment, prayer and action, and sharing.

SUMMARY

1. The staple components of the small Christian community meeting are these:
   • reality
   • word of God
   • community.
2. The meeting ought to be functional, or meet real needs, and flexible.
3. As well as the meetings proper, informal friendly encounters can build relationships. As such we value them.
4. To be meaningful, the word of God must be life-related.
5. Ordinary people are at home with the Bible: its stories, myths, symbols, and songs.
6. A resource person can help small Christian communities by filling in for them something of the historical and cultural background to the Scriptures.

7. Samples, or paradigms, of eight different types of meetings are given and classified as follows:
   - exercise, or group dynamic (two examples),
   - commitment,
   - prophetic,
   - planning,
   - evaluation,
   - ecumenical,
   - worship (two examples),
   - miscellaneous.

9

Pastoral Planning

As a small Christian community grows in maturity, it should feel the need to make a thoroughgoing pastoral plan for its area. But there can be no question of sound pastoral planning unless the community truly knows the place for which it is planning. Merely living in an area doesn't supply the depth of knowledge about which we are speaking. Planning entails understanding the religious, political, social and economic realities of a situation as the ordinary people of a locality see them. To do this, the members of the small community need to make a careful study of the situation. I shall outline a method which in practice I have found effective. I believe that this planning method could be used not only by small Christian communities, but also, with adaptations, by parishes, dioceses or whatever.

Let us presume that the small Christian community has chosen six of its members to form a team to coordinate the pastoral planning process. If there are persons among them qualified in some relevant scientific disciplines, so much the better. These disciplines would be theology, catechetics, psychology, sociology, anthropology and economics. Ordinarily, however, this is not possible, in which case the members chosen will equip themselves through the practical experience of doing the task. Of course it might be possible to co-opt a couple of resource persons from without the community onto the team.

The planning method in question has seven steps that are fairly common to most planning procedures. All the steps are

important to the process, so there should be no short-cuts. The steps are as follows:
1. The team positions itself.
2. The approach.
3. First meeting at grass-roots.
4. Second meeting at grass-roots.
5. Examination of problems.
6. Analysis of systems.
7. An overall view.

THE TEAM POSITIONS ITSELF

First the team positions itself. The members must interest themselves in the total environment of their area. This involves a preliminary survey with instructions and questions that are crystal clear. Such clarity in queries and instructions must characterize the whole planning process. The survey should assist them in getting to know the place better in terms of

- climate,
- boundaries, mountains, hills, ravines (topography),
- rivers, canals, lakes and sea (hydrography),
- roads, rail, electricity, water supply, sewage (infrastructure),
- buses, trains, taxis (transport),
- post, telephone system, newspapers, radio and television (social communications),
- living conditions, ethnic groups, customs, schools and places of assembly (social and cultural factors).

The team is engaged in *pastoral* planning and not in a merely social operation. This first step, therefore, and every step or phase of the planning process, will be done in the light of the word of God and Church documents. And the same will be true of the subsequent implementation.

The reader may be wondering what relevance some of the items listed above have to pastoral planning. The geographical requirements, for example, may seem odd. But these can be truly significant.

I once gave a retreat at a girls' school in a small Irish town through which a river flowed. In the frank atmosphere of the encounter the students admitted that the girls from one side of the river looked down on those from the other. And indeed if the expression "to come from the wrong side of the river" has not entered the idiom of the English language, "to come from the wrong side of the tracks" certainly has.

I also recall a parish where people were divided by a deep ravine, making cohesion and communication extremely difficult.

THE APPROACH

Despite the initial contact made in the foregoing phase, the planning team may not be truly in touch with their people. They must do something to remedy this. In the first phase they will have come closer to some of their neighbors, so they will commence conversing with them and many others on a variety of matters including these:

- the family,
- working conditions,
- cultural events,
- main sicknesses,
- political involvement,
- and religious practices.

From these conversations the team draws up a first version of a list of problems. They must, however, realize that this initial approach will not produce a profound knowledge of the area.

There is a tendency of which the team must be aware from the start. It is a strong inclination on their part to color all the findings with their own way of thinking. In short it becomes a matter of the problems as they see them and not necessarily as their neighbors see them. There has to be a major effort to eliminate this weakness. So the neighbors must be thoroughly consulted.

FIRST MEETING AT GRASS-ROOTS

It is precisely to involve fellow residents and delve deeper into the reality of the place that a first meeting at grass-roots is held. The participants at this meeting will be the planning team, the remaining members of the small Christian community and those neighbors whom the team has come closer to in previous stages.

At the meeting, the participants should be presented with the first version of a list of problems and should be asked to think carefully about it. They may add to or modify the list as they think fit.

The organizers of the meeting have to get beyond the point where the people may be telling them what they think they want to hear – another great pitfall in pastoral planning. This can only be done by establishing trust through patient, prolonged dialogue. It is therefore important to allow adequate time for this.

I recall taking part in this first meeting at grass-roots in a South American *barrio*. It seemed at the outset that the greatest worry of the people was to provide a steeple for the church – in an area where there was malnutrition, astronomical unemployment, lack of education, and prostitution. Lengthy dialogue showed that the steeple was among the least of their felt needs, and 18 years later the church is still without one.

An argument may break out in the course of dialogue. If so, the planning team should pay close attention, because in the course of an argument they may get deep glimpses into the realities of the area.

This meeting ought to provide a second more authentic list of problems.

Incidentally, though this method is based on dialogue, the team may find it convenient here or at other points of the planning process to allow written submissions. These can be anonymous. This might prove helpful to certain shy individuals. Personal attacks, however, and outlandish statements unhelpful to the procedure ought to be discarded.

SECOND MEETING AT GRASS-ROOTS

Up to this point in the planning process, the organizing team, even without knowing it, may be unduly influencing proceedings. So they must try anew to eliminate any possible bias from the proceedings.

Furthermore, people may be shy of each other and of the

team. Time is needed so that all concerned get to know each other better.

To solve such difficulties as these, a second meeting at grass-roots is held. The number of participants is greatly increased from the previous meeting. After a brief introduction and, perhaps, a group dynamic to relate people, they are presented with a second version of a list of problems and are urged to think carefully about it and make the relevant comments.

The planning team must be satisfied that there are a sufficient number of persons present to make the gathering authentic. Following the group meetings a general session is held to pool ideas.

This encounter should root out most of the defects of the second list of problems and lead to a merging of opinions. Items may be dropped, added to or altered. In short the team will likely discover a much more valid catalogue of problems.

And this is also the point in the planning process where we try to identify the generative problems in our list. By generative problems we mean those that give birth to many others. Thus, for example, abject poverty can lead to hunger, disease, crime, prostitution, and so forth.

EXAMINATION OF PROBLEMS

Equipped with the new list of problems and perhaps more importantly with the list of generative problems, the team must now move on to a more profound examination of the situation. Even if they have been proceeding in the planning process without professional help, they would do well to involve some qualified people for this particular phase. But again, this should occur only if it is possible.

So far the team has been dealing with problems as they show themselves outwardly. Indeed, they have been striving to make sense of a most complicated reality. Now they must face an even greater challenge and strive to search out the root causes of the problems under consideration. This they do together with the remaining members of the small Christian community and those of their neighbors who took part in the first meeting at grass-roots.

There are a number of questions which need answering, such as these:

- Is the problem new?
- If not, how far back does it go?
- Why wasn't something done about it long before?
- Has the make-up of people (attitudes, how they see the world, their manner of thinking) anything to do with the problem?
- Can't the authorities, the law or anybody remedy the situation?
- What can the participants of the meeting and people like them do about a solution?
- Do they need to organize?

These and similar questions will lead the planning team and their associates to discover the root causes of problems together with their psychological, sociological, cultural and historical ramifications. They will also discover that they themselves are not without blame where the evils around them are concerned. This will make for more tolerance. And instead of ranting about "they" and "them," they will begin to speak of "we" and "us."

ANALYSIS OF SYSTEMS

The previous stage leads naturally to a consideration of how the society in which we live is organized. This can bring the team face to face with oppressive structures, which cry out for "bold transformations and innovations that go deep."[49] For nearly three decades the Church has been insisting that we must look to the very structures of our society and do something about those. A dab of paint here or a nail there is not enough. Unjust structures divide people into haves or have-nots and condemn millions to real death or a living death through misery, hunger and disease.

And oppressive structures give rise to values, attitudes and actions that are widespread and utterly blighted by selfishness. To deal effectively with these we must get at the causes.

AN OVERALL VIEW

As the team and its associates analyze systems, they inevitably find that the problems that they encounter are widespread. They may have differing aspects from area to area, but basically they are the same. Indeed the evils found in the locality under consideration are to be found in neighboring localities, in the province, nation, continent, and indeed the whole world.

East and West, North and South, people are the victims of powerful structures, preserved by elites who inculcate false values, who gain profit at the expense of people, power at the expense of people. In this they are ably supported by the media. But the great mass of human beings founder in powerlessness and misery. The cause of our time is that of the dispossessed of the earth. Not to involve ourselves is to remain at the margins of history.

Folk can of course feel utterly helpless at the discovery of the power structures that crush the vast majority of human beings. Perhaps such people can find inspiration in the following story.

I once accompanied a group of youth for a weekend's retreat to a place called Riobamba in Ecuador. The retreat was given by Bishop Proaño, who all his life had been a tireless worker for human rights in his own country and in the whole of Latin America. A nominee for the Nobel Peace Prize, he has since died.

Feeling overwhelmed at the weight of the injustices at home and abroad, those young people wanted to know how they could do something about ending them. The bishop went to the blackboard and slowly started to draw. When he had finished, there was the picture of a massive forbidding Wall.

He then went on to ask them whether they did anything to share with their deprived brothers and sisters. They were doing a variety of things: teaching preliterate people to read and write, running a dispensary, counseling children who were glue sniffing, producing a magazine to raise people's awareness of important issues, organizing a club and a summer project for young people.

As they listed their activities, the bishop kept drawing cracks in the Wall. Eventually he asked what would happen to the great barrier of selfishness if good people all over the world, through their sharing, went on making cracks in it. You could actually see the hope dawn in their eyes. It would of course come crashing down.

The message was clear. There was no point in being frustrated by oppressive structures. The thing was to make a crack, even a tiny crack, in the Wall.

The youth in question all belonged to the same small Christian community. This is noteworthy. They had organized themselves to do something about the situation of injustice round about them. And therein lies the secret: We must organize ourselves in the struggle for freedom and justice and make contact with other groups engaged in the same struggle.

PLANNING

As a result of the foregoing steps, the planning team, the remaining members of the small Christian community and other close associates,

- know the locality under consideration well (problems, generative problems, root causes of problems),
- have a more complete vision of the world and how it operates (religiously, politically, socially, and economically),
- feel a need to organize so as to do something about their situation,
- have made a realistic appraisal of resources (human, financial, structural),
- have explored bold and imaginative ways of multiplying these resources (through voluntary help, an animating leadership, service as opposed to finance, making the most of existing premises rather than rushing to build. . .),
- and have grown humanly and spiritually in the course of their endeavors.

In short, they are now in a position to plan. They must decide on
–objectives,
–targets for the objectives,
–and programming of targets.

- Objective: This is a wide statement of the goal one wishes to achieve. For example: *As a community committed to young people, we work with them, and on their behalf for justice.* This objective on justice is taken directly from the provincial pastoral plan of a religious congregation which works with youth.

Many objectives may be listed, but eventually four or five must get priority. These are the ones that will be immediately acted upon. Attempting too much can mean ending up doing little or nothing. Remaining objectives may be filed for future consideration.

- Target: This is a statement which contains a more practical working out of the objective. One of the targets for the objective given above was this: *Education for justice is to be part of initial and ongoing formation at local and provincial levels.* As in the case of objectives, many targets may be listed, but only about ten should get priority (approximately two for each objective). These are the ones for immediate programming and action, while the remainder may be filed for future attention.
- Programming of target: This means making a target still more practical and precise. It involves deciding the
  –WHY,
  –WHO,
  –HOW,
  –WHERE,
  –WHEN
  of the matter. The target just mentioned was programmed as follows: *The Church nowadays has an ever-growing concern for justice; and our founder, St. John Bosco, demanded justice for the exploited young workers of his day. Inspired by the Church and the founder, our Formation Team shall take practical steps to realize the target, at our own centers and those of others, by September 1987. The steps may possibly include organizing*
  –retreats,
  –community, inter-community, regional and provincial gatherings,
  –courses, seminars, lectures, discussions; and providing and suggesting literature and audio-visual material.
  One will have noted how this programming is concerned with specifics:
  –WHY: inspired by the Church and the founder,
  –WHO: our Formation Team,
  –HOW: practical steps are to be taken (examples are spelled out),
  –WHEN: by September 1987.

THE FINAL DOCUMENT

With objectives and targets selected and programming for the targets done, the pastoral plan is ready for implementing.

Apart from possible introductory material, lists of contents, appendices or bibliography, what follows will be the sequence in the document of the plan:

Objective

+

Target

+

Programming of Target

And this sequence will be repeated until all the objectives with their programmed targets are set down.

Depending on the scope of the document, it may be convenient to arrange the objectives, targets and programming of targets under relevant headings, such as *Mission, Community, Worship*.

Possible introductory material might be a foreword or a statement of the desired future. *A Statement of the Desired Future* would be exactly that: an outline of a vision for the future based on the pastoral plan.

IMPLEMENTATION AND EVALUATION

The pastoral plan, of course, must not just remain on paper. It must be resolutely implemented. And it must be frequently evaluated in all its aspects. It must, when necessary, be updated. So there simply must be an animating team that will take regular and precise action to ensure that both are faithfully done. However, everything must not be left to the animating team. The eventual success of the plan will depend on the wholehearted involvement of all whom it touches. All must own it. All must take responsibility for it.

Questions such as the following can help the work of evaluation:

- Have we taken the steps which we determined to take through the programmed targets to realize the objective under examination?
- If not, why not?
- Is there something to rectify?
- Do we need to make adjustments?
- Has there been progress?
- Are we united and organized?
- Do we respect process, yet have a sense of urgency?
- Do we keep in mind that what we are about is a faith exercise?
- Concretely, is what we do illumined by prayer, and reflection on the word of God and Church documents?
- Is there discernment through mature dialogue?
- Is the animating team ensuring that the momentum of the pastoral plan is maintained?
- Is it encouraging the wholehearted participation of all those whom the plan touches?

I might just point out here that a number of small Christian communities may cooperate on the making of a pastoral plan. Or it might be convenient to orchestrate the planning from the parish center. It could even be the case that a pastoral team might come into an area on behalf of the diocese to facilitate the elaborating of a plan. Where a team comes from outside, the members must really struggle hard through the various preparatory steps to get to know the place in question. And, of course, it is absolutely crucial that outsiders relate to and involve the locals in the making and implementing of the pastoral plan.

"To make a ragout you must first catch your hare." So said one Doctor Hill in a work entitled *Cook Book* (1747)[50]—at least the volume was attributed to him. One can imagine old Dr. Hill chuckling to himself as, tongue in cheek, he saw the double meaning in what he had written. Now making a pastoral plan is one thing; implementing it quite another. Implementing it is the pastoral equivalent of catching your hare. I hope the foregoing questions may help people to do so. But where hares are concerned, I prefer my hare running wild and free, thank you, Dr. Hill!

SUMMARY

1. Pastoral planning requires a thorough knowledge of all aspects of a situation.
2. The small Christian community chooses a team (qualified people, but only if possible) from among its members to facilitate and coordinate the planning process. The team employs this seven-stage method:
   - The team positions itself.
   - The approach.
   - First meeting at grass-roots.
   - Second meeting at grass-roots.
   - Examination of problems.
   - Analysis of systems.
   - An overall view.
3. First the team positions itself. The members take an interest in the whole environment of their area. This involves a preliminary survey to get to know the place better: considering climate, physical features, means of transport, means of social communication, social and cultural factors. The questions and instructions for this and all stages of the plan should be clear. The team writes up the results of this initial inquiry and draws a detailed map of the place. Planning at every phase and implementing are done in the light of the word of God and Church documents.
4. The approach: The team converses with various neighbors on matters touching their lives and draws up a first list of problems. The team members identify and strive to eliminate any bias they themselves may have.
5. First meeting at grass-roots: The team members meet with those fellow residents with whom they have conversed so far—to involve them more. They present the first list of problems for their consideration, and help them to be objective—trust is built up through patient dialogue. A second more authentic list of problems emerges.
6. Second meeting at grass-roots: The team strives anew to eliminate any bias they themselves may have and help people grow acquainted with one another. A second grass-roots

meeting facilitates these goals—the number of participants is greatly increased, so as to be adequate and representative. Those taking part reflect on the second list of problems—adding, dropping or altering items. They work in groups and pool ideas in a general assembly. A still more authentic list of problems emerges. Generative problems (those that give birth to others) are identified.

7. Examination of problems: Together with those neighbors who took part in the first grass-roots meeting, the team searches out the root causes of the problems. It would be good to involve qualified persons, if available, at least in this phase.
8. Analysis of systems: The team and its associates consider how society is organized. This brings them into contact with oppressive structures which can only be effectively dealt with in their root causes.
9. An overall view: Looking beyond their own area, the team and its associates see that oppressive structures prevail throughout the world. We must organize in small groups, relate to one another, make our little crack in the Wall.
10. Resulting from the "Steps Towards Planning," the team and its associates
    - know the reality,
    - have an integral world vision,
    - feel a need to organize,
    - have made a realistic appraisal of resources,
    - have explored imaginative ways to multiply resources,
    - and have gained spiritually.

    They are ready to plan.
11. They now decide on:
    - priority objectives (four or five),
    - and priority targets (approximately two for each objective) which they program for action.

      The objectives and targets remaining are filed for future consideration.
12. Objective: This is a wide statement of the goal one wishes to achieve.

    Target: A statement which contains a more practical working out of the objective.

Programming of Target: This means making a target still more practical and precise with regard to persons, places, times, tasks and resources.

13. The heart of the final document lies in the sequence:

Objective

+

Target

+

Programming of Target

until all the objectives, targets and programming for targets are set down.

14. There has to be resolute implementation and frequent evaluation of the plan. There must be the necessary updating. A team takes responsibility to see that all this is done. But success depends on the team involving all the people whom the plan touches in its implementation.

A Word of Conclusion

Thus ends our consideration of small Christian communities. Are they a whole new way of being Church? I think so. Not simply for the reasons, sometimes alleged, that they are emphasizing "community" as opposed to "hierarchy" or "institution" or because of their impressive sharing. These phenomena have been experienced in the Church before, particularly in the early Church. For me the newness lies in the irruption of the poor and the powerless on to the world and Church scenes, clamoring for freedom and participation, their rightful heritage; and in the mold-breaking outreach to what we Christians would call the Kingdom, which is also a marked feature of our times.

Notes

1. Raymond E. Brown, *The Churches the Apostles Left Behind*, New York: Paulist Press, 1984, p. 11.

2. *Revista Eclesiástica Brasileira*, 17, 1957, pp. 731–737.

3. Leonardo Boff, *Ecclesiogenesis: The Base Communities Reinvent the Church*, Maryknoll, New York: Orbis Books, 1986, p.3.

4. Joseph G. Healy, *AFER*, Eldoret, Kenya: GABA Publications, vol. 30, no. 2, p. 76, April 1988.

5. This statistic was given to me by a reliable on-the-spot source.

6. *AFER*, December 1984, p. 377.

7. Paul VI, *Evangelii Nuntiandi (Evangelization Today)*, Dublin: Dominican Publications, 1977, no. 58, p. 31.

8. John Eagleson and Philip Scharper (eds.), *Puebla and Beyond*, Maryknoll, New York: Orbis Books, 1979, no. 96, p. 135.

9. Dr. Ian Fraser of the Basic Christian Communities Resource Center, Scottish Churches House, Dunblane, questions the generally accepted opinion that the small Christian communities began in Latin America. He says that they did not originate in any one country or region, but began emerging worldwide from the 1960s onward as a "spontaneous combustion of the Holy Spirit." Having travelled in 80 countries contacting the communities, he is in a position to know. Reflecting on my own experience, I am leaning toward the view that he is correct.

10. Latin American Bishops, *The Church in the Present-Day Transformation of Latin America in the Light of the Council* (Medellín documents), "Joint Pastoral Planning," no. 10, Washington, D.C. (Secretariat for Latin America, National Conference of Bishops), 3rd ed., 1979.

11. Paul VI, *Evangelii Nuntiandi*, no. 58, p. 31.

12. John Paul II, *The Tablet*, 9 August 1980, p. 787.

13. *Doctrine and Life*, Dublin: Dominican Publications, January 1986, p. 47.

14. *Newsletter* (Salesian), Dublin, December 1979, no. 31.

15. Paul VI, *Evangelii Nuntiandi*, no. 58, p. 31.

16. Dom Helder Camara, *Hoping Against All Hope*, Maryknoll, New York: Orbis Books, 1984, p. 16.

17. J. D. Salinger, *Nine Stories*, New York: Bantam Books, 1964, p. 189.

18. Segundo Galilea, *The Future of Our Past*, Notre Dame, Indiana: Ave Maria Press, 1985, p. 27.

19. Thomas Merton, *The Nonviolent Alternative*, New York: Farrar, Strauss, Giroux, 1980, p. 64.

20. Charles de Foucauld, *Oeuvres spirituelles (Anthologie)*, Paris: Seuil, 1958, p. 166.

21. James P. Grant, *The State of the World's Children* (UNICEF report), New York: Oxford University Press, 1989, p. 31.

22. Paul VI, *Populorum Progressio (Fostering the Development of Peoples)*, London: Catholic Truth Society, 1968, no. 81, p. 38.

23. Austin Flannery, O.P., *Vatican II: The Conciliar and Post-Conciliar Documents, Dogmatic Constitution of the Church*, New York: Costello Publishing Company, no. 4, p. 352.

24. John Raines, personal interview, 15 July 1988.

25. Inculturation of the Gospel, or how to make it flesh and blood in varying cultures, is a burning issue of our time. I think it is quite apparent from this volume that the small Christian communities are powerful instruments for inculturation. This is because of their emphasis on seeing all in the light of their own experiences.

26. Flannery, *Vatican Council II, The Church*, no. 11, p. 362.

27. Paul VI, *Evangelii Nuntiandi*, no. 8, p. 6.

28. Langdon Gilkey, *Message and Existence*, Minneapolis: Seabury Press, 1979, p. 165.

29. William Wordsworth, *Poetry and Prose*, "Tintern Abbey," Oxford, 1921, p. 50.

30. Camara, *Hoping Against All Hope*, p. 19.

31. Raines, personal interview.

32. David J. O'Brien and Thomas A. Shannon (eds.), "Justice in the World," in *Renewing the Earth*, New York: Image Books, 1977, p. 391.

33. Ralph Hodgson, *Poems*, London: Macmillan, c. 1917.

34. Paul VI, *Populorum Progressio*, no. 32, p. 17.

35. Afri (Action from Ireland) Newsletter, *Peacemaker*, Dublin, Christmas 1988, p. 2. (Source of statistics in this section.)

36. *The Tablet*, 5 June 1982, p. 571.

37. *Newsweek*, 21 June 1982, p. 27.

38. Eagleson and Scharper, *Puebla and Beyond*, p. 361. (cf. Poor: preferential option of Church for.)

39. Paul VI, *Populorum Progressio*, no. 32, p. 17.

40. Leon Tolstoy, *Resurrection*, Penguin, 1966, p. 448.

41. James O'Halloran, *Living Cells—Developing Small Christian Community*, Dublin: Dominican Publications and New York: Orbis Books, 1984, ch. 5.

42. Flannery, *Vatican Council II, Evangelica Testificatio*, no. 25, p. 692.

43. Flannery, *Vatican Council II, The Church*, no. 20, p. 372.

44. Ian M. Fraser, unpublished lecture given at La Salle University, Philadelphia, June 1989. See also Ian M. Fraser, *Living a Countersign: From Iona to Basic Christian Communities*, Wild Goose Publications, 1990.

45. John Henry Newman, *An Essay on the Development of Christian Doctrine*, 3rd ed., London, 1878, p. 40.

46. Carlos Mesters, *The Bible and Liberation*, ed. Norman K. Gottwald, Maryknoll, New York: Orbis Books, 1983, p. 122.

47. Ibid.

48. Sally and Philip Scharper (eds.), *The Gospel in Art by the Peasants of Solentiname*, Maryknoll, New York: Orbis Books, 1984, p. 32.

49. Paul VI, *Populorum Progressio*, no. 32, p. 17.

50. Dr. Hill, *Cook Book*, London, 1747.

Appendix 1

A Method for Bible Sharing

The reader may find the following Bible-sharing method helpful:

1. Invite those present to place themselves in the presence of God. Pause.
2. Read the passage under consideration and leave a couple of minutes for people to think about it.
3. Read it a second time and pause once more—three to five minutes.
4. Invite the participants to share regarding what has impressed them in the passage, paying special attention to the issues, questions, and challenges it raises for their lives. There must be no preaching to others.
5. Determine the practical application of the passage for the lives and action of the participants.
6. Finish off by inviting all to pray as the Spirit moves them.

SHORTER FORM

A sharing such as the foregoing would take up an entire small Christian community meeting. When a session is substantially taken up with something else—for example, planning for an activity or discussing a problem—one has recourse to the Bible later in the process. So the format would be as follows:

1. Planning of action or discussion of problem or whatever.
2. Recourse to the Bible to see what light it sheds or what issues and questions it raises in the situation.
3. Decision regarding action.
4. Prayer.

PASSAGES FOR BIBLE SHARING

Church/Community

- Genesis 1:26–27. "Let us make human beings in our own image . . . male and female he created them."
- Matthew 7:15–28. Matthew's idea of Church—false prophets within—a community that *does* the will of God.
- Matthew 8:18–27. Church—a community that *follows* Jesus come what may.
- Matthew 10:5–42. Church *missionary*—God sends Jesus—Jesus sends community to the rest of the world—world must respond.
- Matthew 11:28–30. Church—a community that takes on yoke of Christ—appears heavy—not so really.
- Matthew 13:24–58. Good and bad found in the Church—weeding expeditions dangerous—a sorting out to take place at the appropriate time.
- Matthew 18:7–35. Seriousness of following Jesus—we must go after lost sheep—whole community makes decisions—Jesus present in community—importance of forgiveness.
- Matthew 19:16–30. Give up anything in order to *follow* Jesus.
- Matthew 21:28–32. *Doing* is crucial in the Church community.
- John 15:5–10. "I am the vine. . . ."
- John 15:11–17. ". . . love one another as I have loved you."
- John 17. Gives theology of community—"that they may all be one."
- Acts 2:42–47. The early Christian community.
- Acts 4:32–35. The early Christian community.
- 1 Corinthians 12:14–26. ". . . you are the body of Christ."
- Ephesians 5:29–31. "The two shall become one."

Commitment/Conversion

- Mark 10:17–31. The Rich Young Man.
- Luke 19:1–10. Zaccheus.
- Acts 9:1–13. The conversion of Saul.
- Ephesians 4:1–16. Attaining "to the measure of the stature of the fullness of Christ."
- 1 Peter 3:13–18. ". . . make a defense to anyone who calls you to account for the hope that is in you. . . ."

Dialogue

- Luke 1:26–38. Listening and speaking well.
- Luke 2:41–52. ". . . and his mother kept all these things in her heart."

- Luke 24:13–35. Jesus listens.
- John 4:1–30. Jesus listens.
- Acts 15:1–41. The apostles evaluate.
- James 3:1–12. Listening and speaking well.

ENVIRONMENT
- Genesis 1 and 2. "God looked at everything he had made, and he found it very good."
- Matthew 6:28-29. "Consider the lilies of the field. . . ."

FRIENDSHIP
- Ecclesiasticus (Sirach) 6:5–17; 9:10. ". . . he that has found one [a friend] has found a treasure. . . ."
- John 11:1–44. Lazarus raised from death. ". . . he whom you love is ill . . . Jesus wept . . . deeply moved."

GOD
- Matthew 1:23. Through Christ and the Church (Christian community), God is present in the world.
- Matthew 3:1–17. "It wasn't that a dove descended but like a dove. A dove is a soft and loving animal. It was the love of God that descended on him." (Sally and Philip Scharper, eds., *The Gospel in Art by the Peasants of Solentiname*, Orbis Books, Maryknoll, New York, 1984, p. 22)
- Matthew 6:7–15. "It is a loving name [i.e., *Abba*] that's given to God . . . we don't have to be formal when we chat with him and we give him the name 'papa.' " (Sally and Philip Scharper, eds., *The Gospel in Art*, p. 32)
- Matthew 6:28–34. Abandonment—put ourselves in God's hands.
- Matthew 7:1–5. God would not have us judge.
- Matthew 18:21–35. The Parable of the Unforgiving Servant—our God is forgiving (cf. also Luke 17:3–4).
- Matthew 20:1–16. The Workers in the Vineyard—God's justice much more ample than our notions of justice.
- Luke 10:25–37, The Good Samaritan; Luke 15:1–7, The Lost Sheep; Luke 15:8–10, The Lost Coin. These passages testify to God's unconditional love, compassion, patience . . . loves to the point of foolishness (old man running)—patiently gives the barren fig tree another chance when all others have given up on it—God a loving parent, not a scorekeeper.

JESUS
- Matthew 3:13–15. Baptism of Jesus—"we shall *do* all that God requires."

- Matthew 4:1–11. Temptations—Jesus *does* the will of the Father.
- Matthew 5:21–48. Jesus calls for *more*—the Kingdom demands it.
- Matthew 7:15–20. Jesus a *doer*, a person for others.
- Matthew 8:5–13. For Jesus faith (trust) indispensable.
- Matthew 9:18–38. Jesus a *healer*, a person for others.
- Matthew 11:1–6. Jesus *opts for the poor*—Kingdom breaks in.
- Matthew 11:25–30. Jesus knows the Father—yoke of Jesus may appear heavy, but in reality light.
- Matthew 12:15–21. The *mercy* of Jesus—he "does not break off the broken reed."
- Matthew 16:21–35 (cf. also Mark 8:31–9:1; Luke 9:22–27). Prophecies of the Passion—*suffering* is part of the deal for those who follow Jesus.
- Matthew 18:21–35. Parable of the Unforgiving Servant—Jesus is *forgiving*.
- Matthew 24:29–31. Christ will come again.
- Matthew 25:1–13. The Parable of the Ten Virgins—we must be *ready* for the coming of Jesus.
- Matthew 25:31–46. Jesus' concern for justice—one of the most eloquent pleas for justice in all of Scripture—Jesus is one with the poor and the oppressed—among them we above all find him—same true of God.

• Matthew 26:14–27:66 (shorter form 27:11–54) • Mark 14:1–15:47 (shorter form 15:1–39) • Luke 22:14–23:56 (shorter form 23:1–49) • John 18:1–19:42	The Passion

At this point it might be useful to reread what has been said about Christ and his passion in chapter 3.

Justice

- Exodus 3:1–20. God the liberator.
- Exodus 6:2–13. God the liberator.
- Exodus 22:20–24. "You shall not wrong a stranger or oppress him. . . ." "You shall not afflict any widow or orphan."
- Deuteronomy 10:16–20. "He expects justice for the fatherless and widow, and loves the sojourner. . . ."
- 1 Kings 21:1–16. A grave injustice. (What are the injustices in your own area?)
- Isaiah 3:13–15. Injustice condemned.

- Isaiah 58:1–12. A change of heart, not just empty worship, is called for.
- Amos 2:6–8. "... they that trample the head of the poor...."
- Amos 5:21–24. "Let justice roll down like waters...."
- Amos 6:1,3–7. "Woe to those that are at ease in Zion...."
- Amos 8:4–7. "Hear you who trample upon the needy...."
- Micah 6:8. Do justice, love kindness, walk humbly with your God.
- Matthew 5:27–30. Good must triumph over evil.
- Matthew 5:38–42. Good must triumph over evil.
- Matthew 25:31–40. "... I was hungry and you gave me food...." How we love decides our eternal destiny.
- Luke 4:16–21. Jesus' mission ... option for the poor.
- Galatians 3:26–29. Away with all barriers.

KINGDOM
- Matthew 5:3–12. The values of the Kingdom—turn worldly values on their head.
- Matthew 5–7. Requirements of the Kingdom.
- Matthew 10. The messengers of the Kingdom.
- Matthew 13. Parables of the Kingdom, mysteries of the Kingdom.
- Matthew 18. The position of little children in the Kingdom.
- Matthew 18:21–35. Forgiveness, reconciliation.
- Matthew 24–25. Those who work for the Kingdom must be watchful and faithful.
- 1 Corinthians 15:12–28. There is a tension—Kingdom is here, and yet to come.

LEADERSHIP
- Matthew 20:20–28. Authority is for service (cf. Mark 10:35–45; Luke 22:24–27).
- Luke 10:1–2. Teamwork.
- Luke 22:24–27. Be a servant.
- John 13:1–20. Jesus washes his disciples' feet.

LOVE (CF. COMMUNITY)
- Mark 4:35–41. Jesus calming the storm, "the lack of love in the world, that's the stormy lake." (Sally and Philip Scharper, eds., *The Gospel in Art by the Peasants of Solentiname*, Orbis Books, Maryknoll, New York, 1984, p. 28.)
- Luke 9:10–17. The Multiplication of the Loaves; "... the Gospel doesn't mention multiplication or miracle. It just says they shared ..." (Sally and Philip Scharper, eds., *The Gospel in Art*, p. 42).

- John 13:35. ". . . men will know that you are my disciples if you have love."
- 1 Corinthians 13. "If I speak in the tongues of men and angels, but have not love. . . ."
- 1 John 4:7–21. God is love . . . love of neighbor . . . love drives out fear.

OPTION FOR THE POOR/MISSION (CF. JESUS)

- Matthew 10:5–15 (cf. Mark 6:7–13; Luke 9:1–6). The mission of the twelve.
- Matthew 21:12–17 (cf. Mark 11:15–19; Luke 19:45–48; John 2:13–22). The clearing of the temple—we must not dare use religion or a holy place as a hideaway—"a den of robbers."
- Luke 4:16–21. Jesus is rejected at Nazareth—Jesus' mission: an option for the poor.
- Luke 10:1–20. The mission of the seventy-two.
- Luke 16:19–31. The rich man and lazarus—scraps from the Rich Man's table totally inadequate.
- Luke 18:18–30. The rich man—Jesus against possessiveness—for a restructuring of society on a basis of just sharing.

PARDON (CF. JESUS—MERCY, FORGIVENESS, HEALING)

- Luke 7:36–50. Jesus pardons the sinful woman.
- John 8:1–11. Jesus pardons the woman taken in adultery.

PEACE

- Leviticus 26:3–13. The elements of peace.
- Judges 6:19–24. Peace the gift of God.
- Psalm 35:27. God desires peace for us.
- Isaiah 2:1–5. Turn swords into ploughshares.
- Isaiah 9:5–7. Messiah the Prince of Peace—peace without and in his Kingdom.
- Isaiah 32:16–17. Justice the basis of peace.
- Isaiah 48:17–19. Peace the fruit of obedience to God.
- Isaiah 48:20–22. No peace for the wicked.
- Isaiah 54:13–17. If Israel just, there will be peace and prosperity.
- Isaiah 60:17–22. There will be peace and righteousness/justice.
- Jeremiah 6:13–15. Peace the fruit of justice, not of a lie.
- Ezekiel 13:10–12. Saying there is peace when there is none is to whitewash a crumbling wall.
- Matthew 10:11–13. A greeting of peace, once uttered, has a power of its own (cf. Luke 10:5–6).

- Matthew 26:51–53. Nonviolence (cf. Luke 22:49–53).
- John 14:25–27. Peace of Jesus the only true peace (cf. John 16:33).
- Romans 8:6–8. To enjoy peace you need to be spiritually minded.
- Romans 14:13–19. Peace is right relationships (harmony).
- 1 Corinthians 7:12–16. God has called us to peace.
- 1 Corinthians 14:26–33. Peace is right relationships (harmony).
- Ephesians 2:14–17. Peace is union with God—Jesus our peace—unites us to God.
- Ephesians 6:10–20. Preaching the Gospel brings peace.
- Philippians 4:4–7. Peace of God communicated through Jesus passes all understanding.
- Colossians 3:14–15. We are called to peace because we are one—the body of Christ.

PRAYER/ACTION (CF. JESUS—DOING—DOER)

- Isaiah 29:13–14. Lip service not enough.
- James 2:14–26. "So faith by itself, if it has no works is dead."

PROCESS

- Ecclesiastes 3:1–19. A time for everything.
- Mark 4:1–8. "The plants sprouted, grew, and produced corn. . . ."
- Mark 4:26–34. Seeds slowly growing—The Parable of the Mustard Seed (cf. Matthew 13:31–32; Luke 13:18–19).
- Ephesians 4:1–16. Attaining "to the measure of the stature of the fullness of Christ."

READINESS

- Luke 10:13; 10:23–24; 11:29; 12:16–21; 12:35; 12:43–46; 12:54–56; 12:57; 13:1–5; 13:6–9; 14:16; 14:28; 16:1–8; 17:26–30; 19:5; 19:11–27 (cf. Matthew 25:14–30). (This list is given with the permission of Professor David Efroymson of La Salle University, Philadelphia.)

WOMEN

- Genesis 1. Implies the equality of the sexes.
- Joshua 2:1–24. Rahab astutely saves her family.
- Judges 4:4–23. Deborah savior and leader of her people.
- Ruth 1–4. Womenfolk truly impressive.
- 1 Samuel 19:11. Michal, Saul's daughter and David's wife, saves David.
- 1 Samuel 25:14–42. The discreet Abigail prevents David from wrongfully shedding blood and saves lives.
- 2 Samuel 21:7–14. The devotion of Rizpah.

- 2 Kings 4:8–37. The Woman of Shunem—wisdom and devotion.
- Judith 13:1–20. Judith saves her people.
- Esther 7:1–10. Esther saves her people.
- Matthew 13:33. The Parable of the Yeast—Jesus appreciates the concerns of women.
- Matthew 15:21–28. Jesus heals the woman of Syria (cf. Mark 7:24–30)—Jesus' miracles not just confined to men.
- Matthew 25:1–13. Jesus appreciates the concerns of women.
- Matthew 26:6–13. Jesus anointed by a woman at Bethany—defends her against critics.
- Mark 1:29–31. Jesus cures Peter's mother-in-law (cf. Matthew 8:14–17; Luke 4:38–41). Miracles of Jesus not just confined to men.
- Mark 5:21–43. Jesus raises the daughter of Jairus and heals the woman with a hemorrhage (cf. Matthew 9:18–26; Luke 8:40–56).
- Luke 7:11–17. Jesus takes pity on the widow of Naim.
- Luke 8:1–3. Women listed with the disciples as helpers of Jesus—many later witnessed his death and resurrection—even when men fled.
- Luke 10:38–42. Jesus' deep friendship with Martha and Mary (cf. John 11).
- Luke 13:10–17. Jesus heals woman with the deformed back.
- Luke 15:8–10. The Lost Coin. Jesus appreciates the concerns of women.
- Luke 18:1–8. The Parable of the Widow and the Judge.
- John 4:1–42. Jesus' respect for and frankness with the Samaritan woman—Jesus sends apostles on mission two by two—Samaritan woman alone converts a whole village—Jesus' conduct towards women revolutionary.
- Acts 1:12–14. Women important in Church from outset.
- Acts 12:12. Key role of women in the early Church.
- Acts 16:11–15. Lydia readily hears the word of God.
- Acts 18:24–28. Priscilla and Aquila equal partners in mission.
- 1 Corinthians 11:5. Women pray and proclaim God's word in public worship.
- 1 Corinthians 11:11–12. Woman and man interdependent.
- Galatians 3:26–29. No barrier between men and women—one in Christ—clearest statement of equality of sexes in the New Testament.

YOUTH

- Exodus 2:11–15. The young Moses.
- 1 Samuel, chapters 16, 17, 18. The young David.
- Tobit (Tobias), chapters 1–14. Much to say to the present generations.

- Proverbs 1:8–9; 6:23; 10:1; 15:32; 17:25; 23:25; 27:17. Youth and the family.
- Canticle of Canticles (Song of Solomon), chapters 1–8. A song of human love.
- Jeremiah 1. The young Jeremiah.
- Daniel 13. The story of Susanna (or book of Susanna).
- Ecclesiasticus (Sirach), youth and the school: 1:22–24 (patience); 3:17–20 (humility); 3:21–23 (study of the law enough for the wise person); 3:25–29 (invitation to meditate); 4:20–31 (critical awareness); 5:9–13 (firm in resolution, careful in speaking); 6:2–4 (dominating one's passion); 7:4–7 (no need to be ambitious); 7:11,32 (compassionate); 18:30–19:3 (controlling one's desires); 20:27 (don't be easily influenced); 22:16–18 (reflecting well before a decision); 23:7,12–14 (wisdom in silence); 33:4–6 (be wise and consistent); 37:7–15 (value of God's counsel); 37:16–18 (communication through silence); 38:24–39:11 (eulogy of the teacher); 41:14–42:8 (a middle way between false modesty and brashness).
- Matthew 9:20. Jesus appreciates youthful frankness.
- Mark 5:35–43. Jesus helps the young girl.
- Mark 10:13–16. ". . . whoever does not receive the kingdom of God like a child."
- Mark 14:51–52. Curiosity of the young man in Gethsemane.
- Luke 2:41–52. The young Jesus provokes wonder.
- Luke 15:11–32. Prodigal Son—harrowing experience, conversion.
- John 8:57. Jesus "not yet fifty years old. . . ."
- Ephesians 5:22–6:9; 6:1–4.
- Colossians 3:18–4:1.
- 1 Timothy 2:15; 3:4; 4:12; 5:4,10.
- 2 Timothy 3:15.
- Titus 1:5–6; 2:6–8.
- Hebrews 12:7,10.
- 1 Peter 2:13–3:7.
- 1 John 2:13–14.

} The caring Christian family and community

Appendix 2

Questionnaire for Evaluating a Small Christian Community

(A community may adapt this questionnaire to its own needs.)

(1) Spiritual life

1.1 Do the members have a purpose, or purposes, in coming to the small Christian community?

1.2 Is due importance given to prayer (communal and private), the word of God, and the Eucharist?

1.3 Is the Bible always related to life and its problems and opportunities? Is prayer integrated with action? Does prayer issue in action?

1.4 Is the Eucharist truly a celebration of a unity that exists among the members?

1.5 Have the members a devotion to Mary that is scripturally based and Christ-related?

1.6 Are they trying to do some spiritual reading daily?

1.7 Can they manage to have days of recollection or retreats together?

(2) Sharing (ideas, creativity, intuition, imagination and emotion)

2.1 Do the members of the small Christian community feel a need for self-enrichment or formation?

2.2 Have they had sessions, courses, workshops on relevant subjects?

2.3 Do they learn from the weekly meetings? From casual conversation?

2.4 Are they provided with helpful literature or audio-visual materials (tapes, slides, films)?

2.5 Who is responsible for animating the community in the matter of formation or self-enrichment?
2.6 Does the community make room for and give due importance to imagination, creativity, intuition and emotion in its thinking? Or is everything a matter of cold reasoning?

(3) Human Relationships

3.1 Do the members of the community accept one another as each one is, while allowing themselves to be challenged by the community?
3.2 Do they strive to strike a healthy balance between respect for the needs of the person and respect for the needs of the community?
3.3 Do the desire and will exist to deepen relationships?
3.4 Do the members of the community, animated by the coordinators, talk things over fully and try to come to an agreement as to what should be done?
3.5 Is the animating team of coordinators (better a team than a solitary coordinator) changed with reasonable regularity?
3.6 What qualities do coordinators particularly need? What would the five most important be?
3.7 Does the community maintain good relationships with the pastor, other Christian communities, the parish and with all and sundry?
3.8 What efforts are made to link up (network) with other small communities that work for the Kingdom?
3.9 Does the group have the courage and maturity to face up to and overcome problems, or do problems overcome the group?
3.10 Do the members thoroughly and with reasonable regularity evaluate the whole life of their community? Are there even more regular partial evaluations?
3.11 Do the members socialize together?

(4) The Work (Apostolate)

4.1 Does being in a small Christian community make any difference to the daily life of the members?
4.2 Does the community have a plan of action that responds to the needs of its area?
4.3 Is the community well enough established to engage in pastoral/social analysis so as to set up a thorough pastoral plan for the area?
4.4 Do the members give an account of what they do to the group?
4.5 Does the group support and encourage them in their efforts?
4.6 Do the members continually reflect adequately on what they do

and then strive to go out and do it better?

4.7 Is the community dynamic in its area? Is it a leaven?

4.8 Is it, above all, concerned for the Kingdom and its justice? Has it made an option for the poor?

4.9 Where possible do the members work at least in teams of two?

4.10 Can they manage to do some tasks as a community?

STRENGTHS AND WEAKNESSES

Having finished the questionnaire to their satisfaction, the members might decide the following:

- What are the three main strengths of the small Christian community?
- And what are the three main weaknesses?

ACTION

The members could thank God for the strengths and consider how they might further build upon them. And they could decide upon a limited number of practical steps (in order of priority) that the community might determine to take so as to deal with weaknesses.

Appendix 3

Shorter Questionnaire for Evaluating a Small Christian Community

(Though shorter, this list should be utterly adequate.)

1. Is the community:

- truly a cell of the Church?
- committed (as a community and in its individual membership)?
- sharing all aspects of life: spiritual (prayer, word of God, Eucharist), intuitive (sudden insights), imaginative (dreams for present and future), intellectual (ideas), emotional (feelings, friendships), apostolic (work) and material (goods)?
- integrating prayer and action? Does prayer issue in action?

2. Is the community Trinitarian? That is, are the members united? And do they relate closely?
3. Does it reach out to promote the Kingdom of God and its justice? Does it opt for the poor?
4. Are all the members involved in decision making, that is, do they conduct their affairs on the basis of dialogue and consensus?
5. Do they give due importance to self-enrichment or formation (courses, workshops, retreats . . .)?
6. Do they understand and respect process?
7. Do they relate the word of God to life and life to the word of God?
8. Do they continually reflect on their action and act on their reflection?

Appendix 4

Guidelines for a Workshop on Small Christian Communities

1. The Team: It is better that a team rather than an individual give the workshop. Again, as in coordination, it is a question of witnessing to the principle of community. The make-up of the team should show sensitivity to factors like the following: feminism, ecumenism, variety of experience, variety of disciplines (theological, pastoral, socio-psychological), representation from the locality, lay involvement and so on.
2. Content: Consideration of what small Christian community is, its theology, its relationship with the traditional Church, practical organizational issues and so forth.
3. Methodology: The predominant requirements here are that the session itself be, insofar as this is possible, an experience of community; and that there be considerable interplay between the team and the participants. These objectives are achieved by means of animated input by the resource persons and accounts of actual experiences of small Christian communities. Then follows the reaction of the participants coming from their own experiences. The usual instruments are employed by the team: talks, group work, plenary sessions, audio-visuals, drama, song-writing, prayer and Bible-reflection sessions. Activities commonly found in small Christian community meetings ought to be woven into the workshop. There may also be practical tasks to attend to such as welcoming and enrolling participants, preparing the locale, preparing the liturgy, serving tea or coffee and so on.
4. Better that at least two participants come from the same place than

a solitary person. On returning, they support each other. Before the workshop ends, those taking part should be given the opportunity to prepare an account of what went on, so as to share it with folk back home. Their hope of course will be that those at home will *do* something about it.

NOTE: Sometimes it may be impossible for interested people to find the resource persons to conduct a workshop on small Christian communities. They should not be dismayed, but do it themselves, in which case this volume might serve as a basis. They could proceed as follows:

1. Study one or more chapters at a time; see what questions and issues are raised and discuss them.
2. See if the word of God doesn't shed some light on the questions and issues raised (cf. Appendix 1).
3. Determine what action to take as a result of the foregoing.
4. Engage in prayer.

Annotated Bibliography on Small Christian Communities

Azevado, Marcelo, de C., S.J. *Basic Ecclesial Communities in Brazil.* Washington, D.C.: Georgetown University Press, 1987. A thorough investigation of the "fascinating reality of Brazilian Basic Ecclesial Communities." Geared to the academic.

Baranowski, Arthur R. *Pastoring the Pastors.* Cincinnati, Ohio: St. Anthony's Messenger Press, 1986.

———. *Praying Alone and Together.* Cincinnati, Ohio: St. Anthony's Messenger Press, 1986.

———. *Creating Small Faith Communities.* Cincinnati, Ohio: St. Anthony's Messenger Press, 1988. These three books are related to an experience of small Christian communities in Detroit, Michigan, U.S.A.

Barreiro, Alvaro, S.J. *Basic Ecclesial Communities – The Evangelization of the Poor.* Maryknoll, New York: Orbis Books, 1982. This simply written book shows the power of the poor for evangelization, particularly when this power is harnessed in basic ecclesial communities.

Biagi, Bob. *A Manual for Helping Groups to Work More Effectively.* University of Massachusetts, Amherst, Mass. A book that reads easily and may be adapted for use by small Christian communities; it has useful suggestions for group dynamics or exercises.

Boff, Leonardo. *Ecclesiogenesis: The Base Communities Reinvent the Church.* Maryknoll, New York: Orbis Books, 1986. The author explains in an absorbing fashion how the Brazilian basic Christian communities are a new way of being Church.

———. *Jesus Christ, Liberator.* Maryknoll, New York: Orbis Books, 1978. Refreshing insights on Jesus.

Brown, Raymond E. *The Churches the Apostles Left Behind.* Mahwah, New Jersey: Paulist Press, 1984. In New Testament times, the Church was not a monolith – there were various models operating.

Byrne, Tony, C.S.Sp. *Working for Justice and Peace: A Practical Guide*. Ndola, Zambia: Mission Press, 1988. A practical guidebook for people who wish to encourage and motivate themselves and others to take action for justice and peace.

Cook, Guillermo. *The Expectation of the Poor—Latin American Basic Ecclesial Communities in Protestant Perspective*. Maryknoll, New York: Orbis Books, 1985. A fine, perhaps the finest, academic treatment of basic ecclesial communities in Latin America.

Crosby, Michael H. *House of Disciples—Church, Economics and Justice*. Maryknoll, New York: Orbis Books, 1988. Through an in-depth exploration of Matthew's Gospel and its socio-economic milieu, this book shows how the world of the early Church continues to challenge Christians today. It makes a unique contribution to both New Testament scholarship and the practice of contemporary spirituality.

Dearling, Alan, and Howard Armstrong. *The Youth Games Book*. I.T. Resource Centre, Quarriers Homes, Bridge of Weir, Renfrewshire, Scotland, 1980. Useful exercises for youth.

Donovan, Vincent, C.S.Sp. *Christianity Rediscovered*. Maryknoll, New York: Orbis Books, 1982. A rare book. It really makes one think about Church in a wonderfully creative fashion.

Dorr, Donal. *Option for the Poor: A Hundred Years of Vatican Social Teaching*. Maryknoll, New York: Orbis Books, 1983; Dublin: Gill & Macmillan, 1983. An excellent scholarly survey of the period under consideration.

Dulles, Avery, S.J. *Models of the Church*. Dublin: Gill & Macmillan, 1976; New York: Image Books, Doubleday and Co., 1978. This book shows us that the Church is not just one simple reality, but can express itself in various forms or models.

Eagleson, John, and Philip Scharper (eds.). *Puebla and Beyond*. Maryknoll, New York: Orbis Books, 1979. Included is the opening address of John Paul II to the Bishops' Conference in Puebla.

Éla, Jean Marc. *African Cry*. Maryknoll, New York: Orbis Books, 1986. For me, this book parallels Gutierrez's *A Theology of Liberation*. It does for Africa what Gutierrez's book did for Latin America.

Flannery, Austin (ed.). *Vatican II: Conciliar and Post-Conciliar Documents*. Dublin: Dominican Publications, 1975; New York: Costello Publishing Co., 1975.

———. *More Post-Conciliar Documents*. Dublin: Dominican Publications, 1982; New York: Costello Publishing Co., 1982.

Fraser, Margaret and Ian. *Wind and Fire—The Spirit Reshapes the Church in Basic Christian Communities*. Basic Communities Resource Centre, S.C.C., Dunblane FK15 0AJ, Scotland, 1986. This book gives us the opportunity to feel the life of the small Christian communities. In it the communities speak for themselves.

Fung, Raymond. *Households of God on China's Soil.* Maryknoll, New York: Orbis Books, 1983. A refreshing collection of first-hand experiences of fourteen Chinese Christian communities during the turbulent Cultural Revolution years.

Gaba Publications. *African Cities and Christian Communities*. Spearhead No. 72, Eldoret, Kenya, 1982. A good study by people with first-hand knowledge of the situation.

Galilea, Segundo. *The Future of Our Past.* Notre Dame, Indiana: Ave Maria Press, 1985. One is struck by how relevant the spirituality, or motivation for life, of the great Spanish mystics is to modern times. And it is particularly suited to the small Christian communities.

Gutiérrez, Gustavo. *A Theology of Liberation*. Maryknoll, New York: Orbis Books, 1973. A book that created a watershed in theology.

Healy, Joseph G., M.M. *A Fifth Gospel—The Experience of Black Christian Values*. Maryknoll, New York: Orbis Books, 1981. Gives valuable insights into the workings of small Christian communities in Africa.

Healy, Sean, S.M.A., and Brigid Reynolds. *Social Analysis in the Light of the Gospel*. Dublin: Folens and Co., 1983. A useful work that emerged from a series of workshops.

Hirmer, Oswald. *How To Start Neighbourhood Gospel Groups*. Lumko Missiological Institute, P.O. Box 5058, Delmenville 1483, South Africa. A kit with posters and textbook for learning a method of Gospel sharing. Widely used in Africa.

Holland, Joe, and Peter Henriot, S.J. *Social Analysis: Linking Faith and Justice*. Maryknoll, New York: Orbis Books, 1983. A valuable book by two experienced practitioners. Suited for animators of groups.

Hoornaert, Eduardo. *The Memory of the Christian People*. Maryknoll, New York: Orbis Books, 1988. This book reveals striking similarities between the Church's first communities and the grass-roots communities transforming the Church today. It puts one in touch with useful documentation from the early Church and provides a secure historic base. I found it an excellent and satisfying book.

Hope, Anne, and Sally Timmel. *Training for Transformation: A Handbook for Community Workers*, 3 vols. Gweru, Zimbabwe: Mambo Press, 1984. As well as achieving their purpose, these volumes also provide excellent group exercises or dynamics. Widely used, especially in Africa.

Huelsmann, S.J. *Pray—An Introduction to the Spiritual Life for Busy People*. Mahwah, New Jersey: Paulist Press, 1976 (comes with a

Moderator's Manual). A "course" in prayer to be used alone or in groups. Communities in the United States have found this book most helpful.

John Paul II. *Redemptor Hominis*. London: Catholic Truth Society, 1979.

———. *Laborem Exercens (On Human Work)*. London: Catholic Truth Society, 1981.

———. *This Is the Laity* (Simplification of *Christifideles Laici*). England: The Grail, 1989.

Kalilombe, Patrick A. *From Outstation to Small Christian Community*. Eldoret, Kenya: Gaba Publications, 1981. A most interesting study, adapted from a doctoral thesis, by a person who was himself one of the pioneers in fostering African small Christian communities.

Latin American Bishops. *The Church in the Present-Day Transformation of Latin America in the Light of the Council* (Medellín documents). Washington D.C. (Secretariat for Latin America, National Conference of Bishops), 3rd ed., 1979.

Lernoux, Penny. *Cry of the People*. Middlesex: Penguin, 1981; New York: Doubleday, 1980. An excellent resource book on the National Security State and the role of the multinationals.

Le Shan, Lawrence. *How To Meditate*. Boston: Bantam Books, Little Brown and Company, 1974. A book that has helped many people.

Lobinger, Fritz. *Building Small Christian Communities*. Lumko Missiological Institute, P.O. Box 5058, Delmenville 1483, South Africa, 1981. A kit with large posters and textbook for starting small Christian communities. Widely used in Africa.

Marins, José. *Church from the Roots*, London, CAFOD, 1989. Proceeding from modern day parables, a greatly experienced author draws valuable conclusions for small Christian communities.

McDonagh, Sean. *The Greening of the Church.* Maryknoll, New York: Orbis Books, 1990. Effectively highlights the crucial environmental issue, theologically and practically.

Mesters, Carlos. *Defenseless Flower.* Maryknoll, New York, Orbis Books, 1989; London: CIIR, 1989. Shows how the Bible is used in Brazilian small Christian communities.

National Secretariat and Hispanic Teams. *Basic Ecclesial Communities*. Ligouri, Missouri 63057, 1980. This book is simple, theologically rich, and practical.

———. *Guidelines for Establishing Basic Christian Communities in the United States*. Ligouri, Missouri 63057, 1981.

O'Brien, David J., and Thomas A. Shannon. *Renewing the Earth*. New York: Image Books, 1977.

O'Gorman, Frances Elsie. *Base Communities in Brazil: Dynamics of a Journey*. Rio de Janeiro: FASE-NUCLAR, 1983. An account of Brazilian basic Christian communities by a person who has been deeply involved with them in the *favelas* of Rio de Janeiro.

O'Halloran, James, S.D.B. *Living Cells—Developing Small Christian Community*. Dublin: Dominican Publications, 1984; Maryknoll, New York: Orbis Books, 1984; Quezon City, Philippines: Claretian Publications, 1985. ". . . there is certainly no better or clearer book on the subject in English nor perhaps in any other language either" (*Doctrine and Life*, April 1984); ". . . the most helpful 'how to' book in the lot" (A. Orley Swartzentruber, Princeton pastor).

———. *Pastoral Planning with Tears*. SDB Media, St. Teresa's Road, Dublin 12, Ireland, 1986. ". . . written because of a felt need to aid groups to develop an authentic and useful plan of action" (*Doctrine and Life*, December 1986).

O'Regan, Pauline and Teresa O'Connor. *Community, Give It a Go!* Christchurch: Allen and Unwin, Port Nicholson Press, 1989. A small community of Sisters of Charity are deeply involved in the interesting experience of making their parish in New Zealand a communion of communities.

Paul VI. *Populorum Progressio (On the Development of Peoples)*. London: CTS, 1967; Mahwah, New Jersey: Paulist Press, 1967.

———. *Evangelii Nuntiandi (Evangelization Today)*. Dublin: Dominican Publications, 1977. Commentary by Bede McGregor, O.P.

———. *Octogesima Adveniens (On Social Justice)*. London: Catholic Truth Society, 1971.

Prased Pinto, Joseph, O.F.M.Cap. *Inculturation through Basic Communities: An Indian Perspective*. Bangalore: Asia Trading Company, 1985. The author explores the potential of basic communities to create a Church that will be "deeply rooted in the Indian values of religiosity, poverty, joy and festivity."

Raines, John C. and Donna C. Day-Lower. *Modern Work and Human Meaning*. Philadelphia, Pennsylvania: Westminster Press, 1986. This volume, which deals with social problems in the United States, has the considerable merit of allowing the poor to speak for themselves.

Reichert, Richard. *Simulation Games—for Religious Education*. Winona, Minnesota: St Mary's Press, Christian Brothers Publications, 1975. Useful resource material.

Research and Development Division, National Council of Young Men's Christian Associations, 291 Broadway, New York, New York 10007. *Training Volunteer Leaders—A Handbook to Train Volunteers and Other Leaders of Program Groups*. This work also has helpful group exercises.

Scharper, Sally and Philip, eds. *The Gospel in Art by the Peasants of Solentiname*. Maryknoll, New York: Orbis Books, 1984. This book shows how the Gospels can be used effectively by ordinary people.

SECAM. *Seeking Gospel Justice in Africa*. Eldoret, Kenya: Gaba Publications, 1981.

SHERC Publications. *Handbook of Social and Health Education*. Cork, Ireland, 1978. Another source of helpful exercises.

Torres, Sergio, and John Eagleson, eds. *The Challenge of Basic Christian Communities*. Maryknoll, New York: Orbis Books, 1981. Reflections on basic Christian communities by some of the most eminent people in the fields of theology and pastoral practice from the Third World. Chapter 16 has information on the use of the Bible in basic communities by Carlos Mesters, which is most enlightening.

Vanier, Jean. *Community and Growth*. London: Darton, Longman and Todd, 1979. A veritable gold-mine of reflective and practical ideas on Christian community.

Whitehead, Evelyn Eaton and James D. *Community of Faith, Models and Strategies for Developing Christian Community*. Minneapolis: Winston Seabury Press, 1982. One of the most insightful treatments of pluralism and community.